Connecting with Adolescents in School

Deana H. Young

Rowman & Littlefield Education
Lanham, Maryland • Toronto • Oxford
2005

Published in the United States of America
by Rowman & Littlefield Education
A Division of Rowman & Littlefield Publishers, Inc.
A wholly owned subsidiary of The Rowman & Littlefield
Publishing Group, Inc.
4501 Forbes Boulevard, Suite 200, Lanham, Maryland 20706
www.rowmaneducation.com

PO Box 317
Oxford
OX2 9RU, UK

British Library Cataloguing in Publication Information Available

Library of Congress Cataloging-in-Publication Data

Young, Deanna H., 1962–
  Connecting with adolescents in school / Deanna H. Young.
    p. cm.
  Includes bibliographical references and index.
  ISBN 978-1-57886-266-5
  1. School environment. 2. Teacher-student relationships. 3. Youth and
violence. I. Title.
  LC210.Y68 2005
  373.14'04—dc22

                                        2005003980

This book is dedicated to Amy, Brad, and countless other adolescents whom I might have connected with over the years. I hope that I made a difference. I know you made an impact on my life. Also, to Jonathan, may your healthy connections always be strong. Live in peace.

Contents

Foreword

For most adults, our school days evoke memories of an awkward but largely enjoyable right of passage toward adulthood. However, for those who find themselves disconnected from their peers, school holds no allure. Instead, it simply represents the venue where they will be bullied, ostracized, or otherwise marginalized.

Perhaps like no other event in recent memory, the Columbine school tragedy focused our collective consciousness on the very tangible consequences of lack of connectedness in a school setting. As a fervent advocate of children's rights, I found Dr. Young's work to be quite compelling. Not only do I view school connectedness as an effective means of keeping young people out of my courtroom, I think school connections are crucial to building the leaders of the future. Her commonsense strategies will be important reminders for teachers and key factors for tomorrow's educators to keep in mind. I commend Dr. Young for her insightful analysis of this important topic.

Robert M. Baker
Circuit Judge
Athens, Alabama

Acknowledgments

I am grateful to so many people for helping me write this book. First, thank you to the researchers whose works inspired me to take on this endeavor: Dr. Robert Blum; Dr. Andrea Bonny; Dr. Maria Britto; Dr. Richard Hornung; Dr. Brenda Klostermann; Dr. Clea McNeely; Dr. Tonja Nansel, and Dr. Gail Slap. My gratitude also goes to Dr. Jena Gaines whose editorial expertise has helped me find the right words for my research findings. In addition, my appreciation goes to Lori Thompson who provided her own insight and wisdom about how to connect with adolescents in school.

Many thanks also go to the school administrators and teachers who were willing to share their perspectives on the topic. Special thanks go to my brother, Werner Hollaway, whose infinite knowledge on the subject and encouragement kept me going. I also want to express my sincere appreciation to Judge Bob Baker for his willingness to talk about the importance of school connectedness. Finally, thanks to Jonathan and Greg; without their support, this book may not have come to fruition.

CHAPTER 1

School Connectedness

Although school connectedness is not a commonly used term, its value should not be underestimated. When educators and people outside of the field ask for its definition, the ensuing discussion often brings nods of understanding. Everyone is aware of the importance of student attachment and involvement in school, yet the power of school connectedness for adolescents is not widely known. When I plunged into researching ways of preventing school violence, I was amazed by the vigor of school connectedness and its protective influence on young people. Years after my exhaustive search began, school connectedness remains the most compelling resource for educators to sustain young people.

Strong school connections can prevent teens from engaging in a host of at-risk or unhealthy behaviors, ranging from smoking cigarettes to dropping out of school (McNeely, Nonnemaker, and Blum, 2002). These connections affect school motivation and students' conduct, academic achievement, attendance, alcohol and substance use, mental health, and participation in sexual relations (McNeely, 2004). School connectedness also provides a defense against dropping out.

The National Strategy for Suicide Prevention, 2000 cites school connectedness as a factor in suicide prevention. The strategy was developed by the Substance Abuse and Mental Health Services Administration, the Centers for Disease Control and Prevention, the National Institutes of Mental Health, and the Health Resources and Services Administration (*National Strategy for Suicide Prevention,* 2002). According to those agencies, suicide claims more fifteen- to twenty-four-year-olds than heart disease, cancer, AIDS, and pneumonia combined (*National Strategy for Suicide Prevention*).

Suicide is the third leading cause of death among adolescents in the United States (Ciampi, 2001), and has been linked with bullying and victimization (Hazler, 2000). Bullying and other forms of violence continue to take a fatal toll on our young people. School connectedness, though, provides protection against the devastating effects of all forms of youth violence. More parents and educators should recognize the life-saving role that school connectedness plays in an adolescent's life.

WHAT IS SCHOOL CONNECTEDNESS?

School connectedness deals with students' emotional affiliation with their school: their sense of belonging to a community, trust in school authorities, sense of safety, and confidence in the school's commitment to them. Connectedness refers to the relationship that students have with each other and with the adults on the campus. It is the leading protective factor for adolescents against multiple at-risk behaviors (Bonny, Britto, Klostermann, Hornung, and Slap, 2000).

School connectedness involves the close ties that students develop within their school setting. Those ties influence how invested in and committed to school students become. School ties affect a student's willingness to engage in pro-social or negative behaviors. In the absence of school connectedness, students are at greater risk for experimentation with alcohol, tobacco, drugs, unprotected sex, truancy, criminal behavior, and violence (Bonny et al., 2000). Strong school ties, though, weaken the lure of risky and health-threatening behaviors.

School connectedness is often described in other terms: school community, school bonding, school climate, school attachment, and social belonging (McNeely, 2004). Although these terms are frequently used interchangeably, they do not have the same meanings, nor are they measured the same way. Whatever the terminology, though, school connectedness encompasses all elements related to a student's affiliation with school. Students need to experience a strong sense of community at school in order to establish protective bonds there. In addition, they need to develop a sense of closeness to school personnel and an attachment to school itself (McNeely et al.; 2002; Bonny et al., 2000;

Borowsky, Ireland, and Resnick, 2001). The school climate affects the level of school connectedness and the emotional ties that students associate with the educational environment (Peterson and Skiba, 2001).

The subject has been extensively researched by the National Longitudinal Study of Adolescent Health (Add Health). It examines health-related behaviors of children in grades seven through twelve, with particular emphasis on the social context where at-risk behaviors are likely to occur (Bonny et al., 2000). The Add Health researchers identified school connectedness as a primary safeguard of adolescent health (Bonny et al., 2000). Distinguished physicians, scientists, and child advocates have investigated the link between adolescent health and school-related factors. Results revealed the extent to which schools preserve teen health.

IMPORTANCE FOR ADOLESCENTS

Connections to school are vital to adolescent health, as this age group confronts the dangerous consequences of poor decisions and unsafe behaviors (Lerner, Lerner, DeStefanis, and Apfel, 2001). Adolescents are particularly vulnerable to perilous and unwise choices. The school transitions that occur during adolescence also magnify risk factors. Between middle school and high school, students begin to disengage from school with ever widening gaps in connectedness (Olsen, 2002).

Although it is common for adolescents to become more independent as they mature, the weakening connections between seventh and ninth grade cannot be attributed to developmental issues, because similar gaps are not found in the higher grades. We seem to be losing students in the transition from middle school to high school. By the time some students reach ninth grade, they no longer feel attached to people at school; they have no sense of belonging, and they begin to distance themselves from school, thus becoming more susceptible to risky behaviors (Olsen, 2002).

Weak ties to school can have catastrophic effects for adolescents and their families, especially when the alienated young people turn to violence. In the United States, the proportion of school shootings involving multiple victims increased from zero percent in 1992 to 42 percent in 1999 (Anderson et al., 2001). The school shooters were twice as likely to have been the targets of bullying than were their victims and peers. Alienated and victimized students often withdraw emotionally and eventually disengage from school (Karcher and Lee, 2002). Mulvey and Cauffman (2001) note that low school connectedness, or a poor commitment to school, is an accurate predictor of violent behaviors in the academic setting.

In 1998, the National School Safety Center developed a checklist of characteristics of youth who have caused school violence and school-related deaths since 1992. The checklist was developed to help educators identify potential behaviors that signal that a student might be a danger to himself or others. Indicators include isolation, victimization, bullying, and involvement with a deviant peer group. Students who are not connected to school are more likely to develop behaviors associated with or culminating in school violence.

The stronger their connection to school, the more likely students are to adhere to behavioral standards and to shun risky actions. School connectedness provides the bonds necessary for strong attachment and commitment to pro-social behaviors (Hawkins, Catalano, Kosterman, Abbott, and Hill, 1999). That commitment offers students protections against a range of at-risk behaviors, including aggression and bullying. Building school connectedness will help parents and schools re-establish constructive relationships with students who have been alienated by bullying (Bonny et al., 2000).

The security offered by school connectedness deters students from making choices that threaten their health and safety, if not their lives. Bullying weakens the five elements of that connectedness: closeness, belonging, happiness, fairness, and safety. The indicators of school connectedness were identified by in-depth analysis of Add Health data as researchers sought clues to identify safeguards against at-risk behaviors.

HOW IS SCHOOL CONNECTEDNESS MEASURED?

School connectedness is measured by taking the sum of the School Connectedness Scale (SCS), which is a five-item, Likert scale survey. Students are asked to respond to five statements: I feel close to people at this school; I feel like I am a part of this school; I feel happy at this school; I feel that the teachers treat students fairly at this school, and I feel safe at this school. The students may choose from a number of responses that range from Not at All, which has a score of one, to All the Time with a score of five. The higher the score, the greater the level of school connectedness.

The national average for school connectedness was 3.6 on a scale of 1 to 5 (Blum et al., 2002). My Alabama study of 793 students in fifth through eighth grade yielded a similar average, with eighth-grade students having a slightly lower average of 3.4 (Young, 2004). No schools in the studies of school connectedness had a student body that was totally disconnected from school, nor did the schools have student populations that were universally enamored with school (Blum et al., 2002).

The five-question measure of school connectedness evolved from analysis of the Add Health study which took into account the social environments that affect adolescent health: family, school, neighborhood, and community (Bearman, Jones, and Udry, 1997). The school connectedness questions are derived from instruments in the National Longitudinal Study of Adolescent Health, a program project designed by J. Udry, P. S. Bearman, and K.M. Harris, and funded by Grant P01-HD31921 from the National Institute of Child Health and Human Development, with cooperative funding from seventeen other agencies. Ronald R. Rindfuss and Barbara Entwisle deserve special acknowledgement for assistance in the original design.

McNeely (2004) points out that researchers developed three methods from the Add Health data to examine school connectedness. McNeely et al. (2002) utilized the five-item school connectedness survey in their research. Resnick and his colleagues (1997) designed a survey with eight questions. Moody and Bearman (2002) measured school connectedness with Bollen and Hoyle's 1990 assessment that contains only three items that inquire into social belonging. Other measures of school attachment include Jenkins' (1997) nine-item measure and a combination of three subscales adopted by Hawkins and associates (McNeely, 2004).

While some questions exist as to which measure best determines school connectedness, the five-item scale allows educators to pinpoint the key elements associated with school connectedness: closeness; belonging; happiness; fairness; and safety. Student scores range from five to twenty-five, with the higher score representing the stronger level of perceived connectedness. Lower scores point toward a student who is disengaged from school.

Although many factors contribute to low school connectedness, the impact of bullying is undeniable. Students are more likely to disengage from school as they suffer the physical, social, or emotional toll of bullying. It endangers the connections that students make with school, especially for boys (Nansel et al., 2001).

WHAT ROLE DOES BULLYING PLAY?

The World Health Organization's Health Behavior in School-Aged Children Survey of 15,686 sixth- through tenth-grade students research suggests that boys in higher grades might be more likely to disconnect from school because of continued victimization and bullying (Nansel et al., 2001). My study confirms the link between school connectedness and bullying. In the study of 793 students in Alabama, school connectedness had a negative correlation with bullying and victimization. In the same study, two boys out of the 793 were found to have school connectedness scores of five, indicating no connections to school. Both students had the highest rate of victimization and the seventh-grade student had an equally high rate of bullying behaviors.

When students suffer chronic victimization, they emotionally withdraw from school (Young, 2004). Li and colleagues (1998) note that ongoing victimization contributes to a lack of affiliation among youth. Victimization has a negative relationship with school attachment. My research also suggests that school connectedness predicts the presence and the levels of victimization. Stronger school ties are associated with a lower level of victimization or fear of bullying. Similar conclusions were found in a study of 4,746 seventh- through twelfth-grade students examining the link between peer harassment and school connectedness (Eisenberg, Neumark-Sztainer, and Perry, 2003). Tenuous links to school are related to higher levels of victimization and bullying.

The higher the level of school connectedness, the lower the level of perceived bullying behaviors. By contrast, weak or nonexistent school ties are linked to a greater tendency to bully. In general, aggressive students do not tend to develop close relationships with other students and teachers. They are less likely to feel a sense of belonging to school than are those who are not as aggressive (Voors, 2000). Similarly, alienation from school has been linked to bullying (Dake, Price, and Telljohann, 2003). Both bullying and victimization erode school connectedness.

Victims and bullies alike are more likely to report low levels of school connectedness. Furthermore, there is a clear tendency to be both a victim of bullying and a bully. My study revealed that victimization and bullying were found to have a positive correlation with each other (Young, 2004). Victims and bullies were more likely to experience similarly low levels of school connectedness.

In addition, the tendency to be victimized was connected to the tendency to engage in bullying behaviors. Chandras (1999) indicates that the number of victimized adolescents, who were also bullies, is growing. After experiencing ongoing harassment from peers, many victims become aggressors, seeking out potential victims. Voors (2000) notes that victimized bullies are more likely to express suicidal ideation and carry out violent acts.

Victimized bullies experience the least amount of school bonding, which is consistent with the Alabama research findings (Dake et al., 2003). Although these students may socialize with an undesirable peer group, they feel very little peer acceptance or strong ties to adults. Victims and bullies have the weakest affiliations to school, with victim aggressors experiencing the lowest amount of school connectedness. Victims who become hostile and combative are the most alienated group of students in school (Natvig, Albrektsen, and Qvarnstrom, 2001).

Over 60 percent of all school shooters were repeatedly victimized by other students (Harris, Petrie, and Willoughby, 2002). The chilling result of long-term bullying highlights the need for prevention efforts. The sheer number of children who are routinely bullied amplifies the problem. In the United States alone, as many as 4.8 million children experience some form of bullying every year (Harris et al.).

Students report as many as one in ten of their peers as being prone to aggressive or violent behavior (Bowman, 2002). Although they often know which of their classmates might be the most dangerous, students often do not voice their concerns to administrators, teachers, or parents.

Students may not be convinced that the teachers or administrators would handle the matter effectively. In general, the failure of students to report reflects a fear of retaliation or a sense that the bullies are only making empty threats. Students who threaten revenge, however, are most likely to regard violence as a practical solution.

With the growing exposure to violence through the media, music, and video games, many young people tend to be more accepting of violent behaviors (Price et al., 2002). Violent actions become legitimate means of problem solving and are not viewed as improper or offensive, especially among peers. Adolescent violence is perpetrated more often against family members or friends than against strangers or property (Ellickson and McGuigan, 2000). A young person's use of violence against family members, siblings, or parents, is often predictive of school bullying (Price et al., 2002).

Isolation and disinterest in school are also predictive of bullying (Viadero, 2003). In addition, multiple moves from one school to another increase the propensity for aggressive behaviors among boys, while low self-esteem tends to predict aggressive behaviors in girls (Ellickson and McGuigan, 2000). Weak bonds in seventh grade have also been found to be predictive of violence five years later (Ellickson and McGuigan, 2000). Bullying usually begins early in elementary school and peaks during the middle school years (Voors, 2000; Weir, 2001). Although bullying often decreases by late adolescence, victims who continue to experience chronic harassment become even more withdrawn and occasionally dangerous.

The extensive literature confirms that bullying is a serious health threat in schools throughout the world (Harris et al., 2002; Olweus, 1993). It endangers the psychological and physical health of victims, witnesses, and perpetrators. The consequences of bullying are far-reaching, leaving very few on a school campus unscathed. Bullying prevents school connectedness by alienating students from their peers, teachers, and families.

Drops in academic performance and school attendance are often attributable to bullying (Flannery and Singer, 1999). Bullying is also associated with depression, anxiety, psychosomatic symptoms, and other mental health problems in children (Flannery and Singer, 1999). When schools prevent bullying, educators will be building school connectedness. In doing so, students will be less likely to engage in other unhealthy behaviors.

WHY DOESN'T EVERY SCHOOL FOCUS ON BUILDING SCHOOL CONNECTEDNESS?

Even though establishing connections with adolescents in school is the single most important thing that educators do for young people, its value is sometimes overshadowed by the demands of high-stakes testing. School connectedness does have a positive impact on scholastic achievement, yet the focus on federal- and state-mandated testing dims the significance of fostering strong relationships with students. Higher achievement scores, though, are an outcome of strong school connections. Fostering strong relationships with adolescents has many unexpected academic and health benefits.

No other variable is quite as strong as school connectedness. Its influence is more powerful than family connectedness in steering adolescents away from deviant behaviors. The quality or strength of school connectedness will determine the likelihood of students jeopardizing their lives through actions that put their health at risk (Bonny et al., 2000). Adolescents experience the highest rates of academic success and the lowest rates of at-risk behaviors when they have strong connections to their schools.

The Add Health study, involving 90,000 adolescents, determined that school connectedness led the way in preventing young people from making unhealthy choices. The Centers for Disease Control and Prevention (2001) notes that, regardless of ethnic, socioeconomic, religious, or sexual orientation, students who feel connected to school are more likely to excel academically, and less likely to engage in delinquent behaviors. Despite the overwhelming evidence about the power of school connectedness, not enough schools build upon its energy.

Educators, though, cannot afford to ignore the need to forge strong bonds with students. Those bonds actually offer protective benefits for everyone within the school environment. Understanding school connectedness, then, is critical to adolescents' safe passage to adult-hood. Joe Jackson, a middle school principal in Alabama, summed up school connectedness as "serendipity—the unexpected and the surprising ways we can allow children to connect." School connected-ness is certainly serendipitous.

Most schools are providing a powerful connection for students. Sixty-nine percent of the youth across the United States feel connected to school (Blum, McNeely, and Rinehart, 2002). The majority of teachers intuitively know the importance of building rapport and trust with students. Educators understand the value of a strong relationship with students. Despite their efforts, though, 31 percent of young people across the United States do not have close ties to school (Blum et al., 2002).

WHAT FACTORS DO NOT AFFECT SCHOOL CONNECTEDNESS?

Two facets of education were found to be unrelated to school connect-edness. First, class size does not affect the level of connectedness that students experience; school size, however, does influence school connectedness (Blum et al., 2002). While it may seem that a larger class size might preclude the establishment of close relationships with students, research indicates that this is not the case (Blum et al., 2002). The larger the school, however, the lower the level of school connectedness.

Secondly, school connectedness is not influenced by whether or not a teacher meets the federal definition of being "highly qualified" (Blum et al., 2002). A teacher's educational background and number of degrees have no bearing on a student's affiliation with his or her school. No difference exists between a first-year teacher and a teacher with a master's degree or other advanced degree with regard to building school connectedness (McNeely et al., 2002).

It is important to note that several elements related to the school environment lower school connectedness. Large schools with a high number of retentions, suspensions, rigid policies, and truancy rates will significantly weaken school connectedness among students (Blum et al., 2002). Educators and parents, though, can improve school connections in a number of ways.

HOW IS SCHOOL CONNECTEDNESS INCREASED?

The extent to which students develop strong school connections, characterized by a sense of attachment, acceptance, contentment, fair treatment, and security, depends on several elements. Those facets of school connectedness will be discussed in later chapters. Not surprisingly, all of the components related to school bonding are tools against bullying. School connectedness protects students from dangerous behaviors in and out of school.

In addition to detailing the characteristics of school attachment, this work offers suggestions for building connectedness. My colleague, Lori Thompson, and I are public school counseling veterans who drew from our experience to develop productive approaches to forging alliances with adolescents. I will be sharing some of our insights and suggestions for building essential connections with today's youth. These strategies are based on research and our work with young people. Even though only five strategies are given for each attribute of school connectedness, I am certain that teachers are devising fresh and ingenious ideas to engage students every day.

I hope that teachers will feel validated and make their own list of additional measures they can undertake to reinforce strong alliances with students as they read the following pages. I am optimistic that parents and novice teachers might gain some ideas and inspiration about their powerful role in the lives of young people. I thank anyone who picks up this book; your commitment and passion to help today's youth are evident.

CHAPTER 2

Closeness
I Feel Close to People at This School

How students rank their feelings of closeness depends on their relationships with teachers and friends. The perception of closeness is a cornerstone of school connectedness. Students must feel close to school personnel and their peers in order to develop a strong attachment to the school itself (McNeely et al., 2002; Borowsky et al., 2001). Research revealed that adolescents seek close relationships with their peers while maintaining the need for meaningful ties to their teachers and families (Karcher and Lee, 2002).

Most American middle and high school students feel a sense of closeness to school. Almost 70 percent of the 90,000 students surveyed indicated that they felt close to people in their schools (Blum et al., 2002). How do teachers continue to foster that sense of closeness in the face of ever greater demands? How can they reach the three out of ten students who do not feel connected to school?

Developing close relationships with students involves caring adults. Even though most educators do care about young people, becoming close to students might become secondary to raising test scores. The shift in focus from individual students to their test results might become even more prevalent because of the strictures of the No Child Left Behind (NCLB) legislation (Eckman, 2001). The people who drafted this legislation, however, recognize that undeniable links exist between academic achievement and school connectedness (Morrison, 2001).

Though perceptions of closeness might seem contrary to school administrators' goals for teachers, strong attachments to school lead to improved academic achievement and educational success (King, Vidourek, Davis, and McClellan, 2002; Zeedyk et al., 2003). School attachments yield positive results in behavioral outcomes as well (Hawkins et al., 1999).

Students are more likely to stay out of trouble if they feel close to people within the school environment. Strong ties to school protect and prevent students from engaging in behaviors that place them at risk. They are more likely to want to stay in school and to perform well academically, rather than trying to get out of school by spending time in the nurse's office or not attending school at all (Bonny et al., 2000).

Strong bonds to school have also been linked to greater emotional health (Blum et al., 2002). The stronger the affiliation to school, the more likely a student is to develop positive relationships. The student also experiences a greater sense of well-being. Dr. Blum notes that socialization is a basic function of healthy middle school life. When middle schoolers expand their network of friends to include students from all lifestyles, their sense of closeness to others increases.

Adolescents, though, can be difficult to reach. Even parents sometimes have a hard time communicating with their teenage children who are often characterized by aloofness or estrangement from adults. Difficulties are multiplied for teachers because they are trying to establish a relationship with all twenty-five students in each of their three, four, five, or six class periods per day. As adolescents grow older, they listen to their peers more than to adults.

Teenagers, though, still need to know that the important adults in their lives can be counted on for support. As they become more independent, adolescents question authority and formulate their own opinions. In order to foster closeness with teens, adults within the school setting must give the young people a sense of security and comfort.

Although class size has been found to be unrelated to school connectedness, teachers may have a more difficult time getting to know students in large classes very well. Classroom management may also become more problematic with a larger number of students. The increased number of students in a classroom takes a toll on school connectedness. Schools that exceed six hundred students have lower levels of school connectedness (Blum et al., 2002). Teachers in smaller schools can develop a stronger bond with more students.

Even though achievement may be higher at schools with student populations of six to twelve hundred, larger schools are not the best places to foster connections with students (Blum et al., 2002). In their book, *And Words Can Hurt Forever* (2002), Garbarino and deLara discuss the melee that can occur on a large campus. Students are also keenly aware that they can become lost on a sprawling school campus.

Young people very quickly lose their sense of self, security, and closeness and become overwhelmed by the sheer size of a large school. Getting close to students on a huge campus is problematic at best and impossible at worst. Reaching young people, especially when almost one-third of the student body may not have any close ties to school, can be a daunting task. Yet the protective power of school connectedness is far reaching.

Educators continually deal with students who are at-risk of falling between the cracks. The teachers can often identify students who are neither close to their peer groups nor connected with any teacher or adult on the school grounds. Those students are at greatest risk of becoming involved with alcohol, drugs, delinquency, and violence. At times, those perilous behaviors even cost students their lives.

School connectedness is one of the keys in protecting our young people from dangerous situations. Developing a relationship with an adolescent, though, can be challenging, especially when that student is on the fringes of the mainstream student population with behaviors or attitudes that alienate others. These students frequently provoke their peers who victimize and ostracize them (Marshall, 2000; Olweus, 1993).

Disconnected students are not members of the most popular groups, nor do they take part in school activities. Their grades are often poorer, and they are more likely to be frequently absent. Victimization often interferes with the student's ability or desire to establish close ties at school. These students comprise the 31 percent of students who do not feel strong connections to school. These youth are the students that schools are losing and must strive to recover.

While educators have overwhelming responsibilities, developing close ties with students improves their chances for academic success and positive peer relations. It is a win-win situation for students and teachers. When school connectedness is strong, students are committed to school. Teachers routinely frame school commitment from students in very simple ways.

In fact, the elements that help build school connectedness are so natural for most teachers that it almost seems unnecessary to give suggestions. That is, however, what trivializes the influence of school connectedness. It is taken for granted that everyone on a school campus is connecting with students. The importance of whether or not a student feels close to people at school is overlooked.

Below are some of the suggested actions to cultivate closeness with students. Developing rapport with teenagers is not tedious nor difficult. It can lead to one of the most fruitful relationships in an adolescent's journey to adulthood. Becoming close to young people primarily involves listening to the students and engaging them in conversations about themselves.

BE ATTENTIVE

Being attentive to students involves listening, observing, and empathizing. Empathy is a cardinal feature of attentiveness. Having an empathetic listener allows students to voice concerns without fear of judgment or reprisal. Teachers must also be sensitive to students' verbal and nonverbal cues. These cues will reveal when something is interfering with the social, academic, or emotional functioning of students.

The student with weak ties to school may be withdrawn and isolated from peers. In addition, the disconnected student may frequently be absent, have repeated a grade, or be unmotivated. When these indicators are present, teachers must be vigilant about changes in behavior, attitude, or demeanor. Being mindful of such changes, conveying concern and caring becomes critical.

Teachers must be unequivocal against racial slurs or negative comments about body size, gender, or socioeconomic status (Weinstein, Curran, and Tomlinson-Clarke, 2003). Such harassment diminishes feelings of attachment that students might develop toward school. In addition, students who feel persecuted may have trouble establishing close ties with anyone. They are more likely to disengage and drop out of school.

Letting students know that teachers understand what they are going through opens a window to a relationship. The stronger the relationship becomes, the more learning takes place. Dedicated teachers are attentive and honest with their students. These qualities attract teens to education. Captivated by the learning experience, these students begin to enjoy school. Rather than disengaging, the young people begin to set career goals and outline a plan for their future.

VALUE EVERY STUDENT

Teachers must affirm, respect, applaud, appreciate, commend, and treasure students; in short, acknowledge each student in some way. Teachers must endeavor to find the value in each student. Students need to feel accepted, believed in, recognized, and trusted. Renowned educator Marva Collins said, "There is a brilliant child locked inside every student." Teachers must mine that brilliance and ensure that each student realizes his or her unique potential.

In *A Nation Deceived: How Schools Hold Back America's Brightest Students*, Colangelo, Assouline, and Gross (2004, Vol. I) note that educators often neglect the needs of students, including gifted students. The authors further note that teachers might overlook their talented students because No Child Left Behind legislation focuses on students who need to acquire basic skills.

Gifted, talented, and creative students, though, can be found in every gender, race, and lifestyle, yet their worth is often overlooked (Colangelo et al., 2004, Vol. II). When all students feel that their presence is valued, they are more likely to devote more time to school. Even though contributions of individual students tend to be lost in larger schools, teachers have the opportunity to recognize and value students within their classrooms (McNeely et al., 2002). The number of students in each class does not affect school connectedness.

When students know that a teacher genuinely cares about how they are doing, they perform better. It is important for schools to affirm the backgrounds of all students in order to promote tolerance and acceptance (Henze, 2001). School connectedness grows when students develop friendships across racial and ethnic lines (Blum et al., 2002).

Having a diverse student population allows schools to build community among students.

Students can still develop a sense of closeness with teachers and their peers if they see that each plays an important role. When teachers see value in every student, students perform better. The students need to know that they are significant members of the school and that they matter. Teachers will gain commitment from students when they value each student's presence.

Blum et al. (2002) notes that a teacher's acknowledgement of students is an indicator of a well-managed classroom. Such acknowledgement also conveys meaning to the students. They get the sense that being there makes a difference and that their voice matters. When students feel insignificant, not listened to, or inconsequential, their participation begins to decline, and so does their attendance. Truancy is associated with how students feel about school. If they feel insignificant at school, their motivation to attend will wane.

CONVEY CONCERN

Educators need to convey their concern for students. I have worked with very few teachers who were not concerned about their students. Teachers worry about students' home lives and whether the families had enough food and support throughout the holidays and school year. Many teachers express their apprehension about possible problems at home and other issues affecting students. Students need to know how much their teachers care about them. Demonstrating that care and concern gives hope to students in desperate situations.

Displaying compassion and interest in students contributes to their sense of closeness at school. When educators acknowledge student opinions and recognize their feelings and perspectives, young people become more attached to school. Teens need to be listened to and heard. Permitting students to express their concerns allows them to work through issues that interfere with their schoolwork and relationships. The social climate is improved when teachers listen to their students rather than just meting out judgments based on their own beliefs (Holtappels and Meier, 2000).

Listening to these viewpoints takes time and attention. It may be difficult for teachers to give students their full attention. Educators may sometimes feel like crisis managers who do not have time for conversations that do not involve academic pursuits or emergencies. Most counselors certainly feel this way. Simple, unrushed conversations with students, though, can nurture a closeness that may very well save one of their lives.

ADDRESS DIFFICULTIES

Teachers often know when students are having learning, emotional, or social problems. Such recognition requires action and engagement with students (Holtappels and Meier. 2000). Although educators are not expected to be counselors, ignoring warning signs of problems may have grave consequences. Although students should be encouraged to discuss their feelings, teachers often do not have the time to do so.

Teachers must take note and action when a student has a problem that should be brought to the attention of the school counselor. As a school counselor, I know that such a referral demonstrates genuine concern. When a teacher tries to deal with the problem alone, the student does not have the opportunity to benefit from the expertise of the counselor. In addition, the counselor can take the time to help students understand their behaviors, expectations, feelings, and responses to various situations (Flannery and Singer, 1999). The door, then, is opened for teaching coping skills, healthy problem-solving strategies, and social skills.

The 2001 national standards for school counseling programs cited effective programs as those that had procedures in place for helping troubled students. Those procedures include offering support for students to improve attendance, concentration, achievement, and peer interaction. Problem-solving techniques and goal-setting strategies are also areas that can be addressed with the school counselor.

In addition, the counselor should be able to devote more time to deal with student problems. The guidance office will also have the means to access community resources for students and their families. Counselors help students overcome obstacles that interfere with their learning. Assisting troubled children requires timely intervention and collaboration among teachers, counselors, parents, and community resources (Dwyer, Osher, and Warger, 1998).

Through a variety of techniques, from individual and group counseling to guidance lessons, counselors help students develop a greater self-awareness (Chandras, 1999). In addition, counseling services also help build resiliency, coping techniques, and school connectedness. Sound guidance programs also promote positive social support among students.

RECOGNIZE STUDENT INTERESTS

Recognizing student interests will draw the young people closer to the school staff and learning environment. Most adults feel closest to people who take an active interest in their lives. Young people are no different. Students need to know that they are more than just names in a teacher's grade book. The quality of the student-teacher relationship affects student learning and achievement (Holtappels and Meier, 2000). When teachers regularly ask their students to talk about themselves, students are apt to pay closer attention in class, behave better, and experience greater academic success.

Teachers with a sincere interest in the students can engage their students more. In other words, students become more interested in what is going on in the classroom when they think that teachers and peers are interested in them. In addition, tapping into student interests helps students become personally invested in school.

I know of one school administrator who assigned one adult mentor for every student on the campus. That mentor's job was to make contact with the student on a daily basis and demonstrate an interest in that student's life. Increasing the number of opportunities for connections to be made is invaluable. Some principals and teachers will make a point of riding the buses so that they know where all their students live. Others will make home visits to meet students' parents and their families. There are so many ways to take an active interest in the lives of students. That interest demonstrates a commitment to students that is often reciprocated.

Fostering a sense of closeness with students helps build strong relationships with them. Those strong relationships, in turn, produce high academic and strong school commitment. Students are happier, healthier, and are able to cope better when they have strong relationships with their peers and adults on the school campus (Karcher and Lee, 2002). The committed relationships they form also contribute to a sense of school belonging. Students want to connect, to belong, to feel like they are important members of the student community. Developing closeness to school complements students's need to belong there.

CHAPTER 3

Belonging
I Feel Like I Am a Part of This School

The need to belong is one of the most basic human needs (Vander Zanden, 2000). It is no surprise that feelings of belonging are essential to building school connectedness. Adolescents need to feel like they belong in school in order to forge a connection to school. Their need for social support is paramount to the establishment of healthy school connections. Without those vital social links, students in the middle grades are more likely to become withdrawn, depressed, and anxious (Karcher and Lee, 2002). If middle school students do not develop a strong affiliation with school, they are less likely to be committed to school and more likely to drop out.

Young people need a strong connection with both their peers and their teachers (McNeely et al., 2002; Karcher and Lee, 2002). Dr. Barry Carroll, an Alabama county school superintendent, noted that students who do not become involved at school might not develop a strong sense of community in adulthood. That sense of community is built through group membership and involvement in extracurricular activities. Student programs should create opportunities for students to be involved as participants and spectators. Carroll noted that such programs, of course, should be balanced with high academic standards. Strong school connectedness is linked to higher scholastic accomplishments.

My brother, a Florida public school administrator, Werner Hollaway, commented that helping students to belong is a hallmark of a good teacher. Despite the growing number of obstacles that teachers face, good teachers are creating a sense of belonging among students by carrying out routine actions every day. These school professionals know the intrinsic value of connecting with students.

Hollaway echoed the beliefs of Morrison (2001) by saying that schools are supposed to be helping students feel a part of something, connecting with them, and protecting them. School connectedness is a serendipitous reminder of why people become teachers: to help children lead healthy, productive lives as adults. Educators' commitment to students creates a safe bridge for them to cross, leaving risky behaviors behind. Their dedication is often tested by an increasing number of hoops that they must jump through in order to prove that they are doing a good job.

Teachers overcome many barriers every day to develop relationships with and among students. By doing so, high standards for academic performance are often reached, not overlooked. Accountability standards are not ignored when relationships with students are seen as integral parts of the educational process. Nurturing a student's affiliation with school generally involves conveying an interest in each student. The strategies below help students feel like they belong at school.

ENCOURAGE PARTICIPATION

Students need encouragement to participate in classroom activities, school programs, or clubs. Stimulating student interest also calls for participation on the teacher's part. Teachers can encourage students to participate in activities by attending student functions. An educator's presence at a student activity is an important one, but many teachers are unable to attend student functions outside of school because of their own family obligations. Doing so, though, tells students that they matter. Demonstrating an interest in students as people also makes a significant contribution to the climate of the school (Holtappels and Meier, 2000). Students and parents alike are impressed when a teacher or administrator takes the time to attend an activity outside of school hours.

If teachers cannot attend the activities, they can acknowledge student participation by clipping and displaying newspaper articles about the events. Interest can also be communicated by asking the student about the activity, ball game, competition, or event. Students can also be asked to share their experiences with the rest of the class. Overcoming student apathy begins with taking an interest in students' lives inside and outside of school. Taking the extra time to focus attention on student activities actually builds strong ties with students.

PROMOTE PARENT INVOLVEMENT

Promoting parent involvement entails ongoing communication between parents and school staff. Positive parent involvement is the number one indicator of a student's success in school. It is especially important for adolescents as they make the transition from primary to secondary school (Zeedyk et al., 2003). For most young people, the school transitions are fraught with anxiety. Contact between the home and school, thus, becomes a critical means of ensuring a safe passage from the lower grades to advanced grades. A student's academic progress and well-being hinge on a successful transition from one school to another (Zeedyk et al., 2003).

Family connections have a decisive influence on both scholastic achievement and school bonding. Pragmatic families often view the association between home and school as vital; overindulgent parents sometimes undermine the efforts of educators. In addition, parents who are too protective or restrictive do not recognize warning signs of trouble ahead. High student achievement is linked to constructive parent involvement (Desimone, 1999).

The partnership between educators and parents increases the potential for students to maintain healthy connections at school. Parents who are actively involved in school functions become better advocates for their children. Adolescent risk factors also decline with strong parental monitoring of adolescent activities, peer relationships, and academic progress (Eaton et al., 2004).

Parental support of school is also critical for healthy adolescent development (King et al., 2002). The strength of family connections is predictive of healthy adolescent behaviors; stronger ties help build coping skills and resilience for youth (Why do some people drink too much, 2000). A strong link between home and school doubles the protectiveness for problem behaviors and is a key factor in violence prevention (Lamberg, 1998).

In order to increase parent involvement, teachers can engage parents through notes home, telephone calls, or through face-to-face conversations. Newsletters, school websites, and e-mail also provide ways to reach out to parents. The more positive contacts that teachers have with parents, the more support parents will give to the educational process. The quality of the parent contact, along with consistent communication, makes a difference.

Parents have suggested that contact be maintained throughout the academic year, not just when there is a problem or at exam time (Zeedyk et al., 2003). Parents have an indispensable role in their adolescents' education, especially as their children begin to assume more and more responsibility for their own education. Parents can support the self-management, self-monitoring, and pro-social behaviors of their teens (Mather, 2001).

Parents who are actively involved in their teen's education also get to know his or her friends. Those parents are also more likely to convey the importance of education and discuss issues related to school and peer groups (McNeal, 2001). Parent involvement also promotes positive behaviors among young people. The more interest that parents have in school, the more likely a student is to enjoy school by becoming more involved with school-related activities.

SPONSOR EXTRACURRICULAR ACTIVITIES OR CLUBS

Sponsoring extracurricular activities or clubs will increase opportunities for students to see that they are an important part of the school community. Students themselves have reported that they feel like a part of the school when they are involved in school activities. The young people realize that their involvement in school increases their chances to become more acquainted with faculty members and other students. In addition, clubs and extracurricular activities allow students a chance for expression that they might not have in the classroom. Through club membership, students can express and put into action their opinions about various social issues. Student-led activities and projects generate a sense of responsibility, commitment, and closeness to school.

The more opportunities that students have to be involved, the less likely they are to withdraw from school. Participation in extracurricular activities and clubs promotes school connectedness among all students. In their study, Renzulli and Park (2002) determined that gifted students who dropped out of school had limited participation in extracurricular activities. Students who actively take part in sports, band, or other student organizations are more likely to establish positive relationships at school.

Participation in sports, in conjunction with other activities, increases the likelihood of involvement in other healthy behaviors (Harrison and Narayan, 2003). Students are more likely to exercise, have a nutritious diet, and do their homework when they are actively involved in some athletic or social organization.

Extracurricular activities may take place during or after school hours; the benefits are the same. Connections to school increase with participation. Research supports the fact that participation in activities such as athletics decreases the likelihood of dropping out (Alspaugh, 1998). Students develop strong relationships with members of the group as well as with group leaders or sponsors. Even though club sponsorship is time consuming, the rewards are many, especially for the students.

Schools that strive to build close ties with students increase opportunities for students to connect with their peers and teachers through extracurricular activities and mentoring (Blum et al., 2002; King et al., 2002). These activities range from sports and cheerleading to academic and service learning clubs. Financial costs for participation in some of the activities, however, can be in excess of one thousand dollars, as with some cheerleading groups. Fundraisers help offset some of the expenses, but parents and students shoulder the main burden for these activities.

Many students may not be able to afford to participate in some activities for financial reasons. Others may not have the necessary transportation. These problems are especially prevalent in rural schools that have a large number of students riding the bus. Some schools overcome that problem by having club meetings during the school day, either during lunch period or according to a monthly club schedule. Schools also offer a variety of clubs or groups for the students.

SUPPORT SERVICE LEARNING AND VOLUNTEERISM

Students need meaningful social involvement (Blum et al., 2002). Service learning and volunteerism improve the odds that students will engage in other healthy behaviors rather than in dangerous ones. Incorporating service learning programs into classroom instruction gives students the opportunity to develop a sense of responsibility for the world around them.

Service projects allow young people the chance to contribute to the world. Supporting these volunteer projects improves attendance, raises academic performance, and promotes character development (Taylor and Larson, 1999). In addition, students develop a sense of ownership and pride in their accomplishments through their volunteer efforts on the school campus and in the wider community.

Service learning can take the form of campus recycling projects that foster environmental awareness or ongoing assignments in soup kitchens, food banks, or other volunteer programs. One powerful service-learning tool involves planning a hunger banquet wherein students learn about issues relating to hunger, poverty, and resources. More information about lessons on hunger can be found at www.oxfam.com or other sites that deal with hunger, poverty, or youth volunteerism.

These types of activities increase not only social and political awareness, but also empathy. Students learn about the challenges that different groups of people face through hands-on activities and projects that they research and develop themselves. In *Nobody Left to Hate,* Elliot Aronson points out the benefits of cultivating empathy in students. Aggressive behaviors decrease while cooperative learning increases when students are empathic with one another. Aronson (2000) also notes that cognitive skills improve as students learn to put themselves in other's shoes. In addition, self-esteem grows.

One empathy-building activity involves the Kindness and Justice Challenge conducted by Do Something (www.dosomething.org). Students are challenged to perform as many acts of kindness and justice as they can within a two-week period in honor of Dr. Martin Luther King, Jr. This activity can serve as a springboard for students being kind, generous, compassionate, and understanding for the rest of the year. With the emphasis on what they can do for others, students are empowered to do more.

Every year I am amazed by the altruism of young people. Students inspire me and other adults with their selfless acts. The Internet offers a wealth of information about integrating service projects into the curriculum. Teachers can find many activities that will fit into the instructional process. Intergenerational programs that link older adults with young people are very beneficial. Such programs have reciprocal benefits for participants that can lead to mentoring relationships.

DEVELOP MENTORING PROGRAMS

Developing and implementing mentoring programs entail preparation, training, and monitoring. Students with mentors are less likely to engage in weapon-carrying and using alcohol, drugs, and tobacco (Beier et al., 2000). Support from caring adults nurtures the adolescent's desire to learn. Mentoring is also a bulwark against other negative behaviors, especially early sexual practices (Beier et al., 2000). Peer mentoring contributes to self-esteem and higher achievement. Students who have mentors are less likely to engage in aggressive acts and to associate with negative peer groups (King et al., 2002). All types of mentoring programs help students strengthen their attachment to their school, peers, and families (King et. al., 2002).

Mentoring programs, though, are fraught with challenges. Adult mentors must undergo a thorough background check. In addition, mentors must be reliable and compatible with the mentees in order for the relationship to benefit the adolescent. Research indicates that a mentoring relationship lasting fewer than ninety days can be harmful to the young person (Novotney et al., 2002).

Nevertheless, mentoring can be an invaluable connection for young people. Increased opportunities for involvement and interaction create healthy avenues in school. Young people become more attached to the people in their school as they are given more chances to form healthy alliances. Close relationships in school also create happiness and satisfaction with school.

CHAPTER 4

Happiness
I Am Happy to Be at This School

Happiness is that feeling of contentment that adolescents rarely seem to express, especially about being at school. Or do they? Add Health results revealed that out of 90,000 seventh through ninth graders surveyed, 69 percent were happy or at least satisfied to be at school. It can be a realistic goal to strive to make students content with their school, but where do those feelings rank when schools are being scrutinized on test scores rather than on the strength of their connections with students?

No Child Left Behind (NCLB) success stories involve schools with below average test scores rising to well above average ratings. While achievement scores might improve throughout the school, the students no longer have recess, field trips, and other experiences that foster contentment and excitement about learning. The social costs of implementing the NCLB legislation can be high when considering the loss of spontaneity and learning experiences traded for practice on standardized tests.

Schools should offer a balance between academics and activities that help young people want to learn even more. Putting too much emphasis on one element at the expense of the other causes everyone to lose, most of all the students. Young people who are miserable are not learning, but just biding their time. Colangelo, Assouline, and Gross (2004) caution educators that they will lose some of their best and brightest students by just having them do "seat" time in class. Research conducted by Renzulli and Park (2002) confirms that fact. Five percent of the gifted students in their study dropped out of school, noting that they were unhappy and did not feel challenged or engaged in school in any way.

It is difficult to imagine that any educator, or parent, would argue that a child attends school to be educated. Increasing student satisfaction with school does not mean that some scholastic pursuits have to be sacrificed. What it does mean, though, is that teachers are helping students to enjoy being in school. These teachers are also contributing to a school climate that is conducive to learning. Some of their tireless efforts at connecting with students will include the tips that follow.

MAINTAIN A POSITIVE OUTLOOK

Maintaining a positive outlook will help teachers do a better job. It is no secret that job satisfaction affects job performance. Discovering ways to enjoy teaching, in spite of all the additional paperwork, requirements, and governmental demands, will help students connect to school. Ultimately, effective teaching will protect teenagers from risky behaviors and engage them in healthy ways. Instead of viewing school connectedness as yet another burden, teachers need to take heart in the awareness of their awesome responsibility.

In order to remain positive, teachers must relax. Relaxing is often a difficult concept for teachers to grasp, especially during testing time. Teachers feel obligated to meet the demands of the community, the state, and the nation's policymakers to have ever higher test scores at any cost. Under those kinds of constraints, advising teachers to relax seems nonsensical, but unless they do, the students begin to feel the same pressure. As tensions mount, the classroom climate can become stifling. Test scores rarely go up under that kind of pressure. The pressure to achieve paralyzes student success (Holtappels and Meier, 2000; Price et al., 2002).

Instead of transferring their anxiety to students, teachers should stay calm while emphasizing achievement. Students are often directed to relax during exam time in order to put forth their best effort. Trying to control their own anxiety can be a formidable task for young people when the adults on campus are stressed or burned out.

Middle school teachers also encounter special challenges that contribute to their own apprehension. Their class loads can affect their ability to reach students.

Educators have much less time to cover more material with growing numbers of students. Although class size is unrelated to school connectedness, the number of class changes during the middle school day can undermine teacher effectiveness. Despite their limited time with students, the middle school teacher remains a dynamic force in the lives of adolescents. Presenting a tranquil demeanor will help students regulate their own emotions amidst all the changes they are undergoing. Such an instructional approach can build connections with students that benefit everyone.

When teachers put themselves in the students' shoes, they capture student interest in a subject. Those teachers enjoy seeing the light bulb go on. In addition, that enjoyment transmits to the class. When teachers tap into the creativity of their students, everyone laughs and has fun. The energy in the classroom is palpable and can be sensed the minute a student walks into the class. Lively discussions often ensue and learning takes place in a spirited atmosphere.

As middle school teachers prepare students to enter high school, the students are often expected to behave like young adults. Despite the perception, though, some middle schools focus on control and discipline (Baer, 1999). Humor and laughter fall by the wayside when rigid policies are sapping student spirit. While adolescents are striving to become more autonomous, strict teacher control stunts that developmental need for autonomy. When teachers remember that adolescents are on their way to becoming adults, the path is a little easier to follow.

Teachers can also lighten the way by infusing humor and imagination into their lessons. Daring the students to think critically and to develop reasoning skills does not have to be a dry experience. Animated instruction does not take a costly toll on teachers; its profit outweighs the cost. Combining teaching methods will increase the likelihood of reaching everyone in the class. Activities that inspire students to think for themselves can also be enjoyable and engaging.

Using humor at the appropriate times can be a very useful tool for teachers. Laughing at the wrong time or when a student makes a mistake can have the opposite effect. If used inappropriately, humor can devastate a student's self-esteem. When used to humiliate and denigrate students, it inflicts wounds that may take years to heal. Ill-timed humor reduces teacher effectiveness. Classroom management also suffers, along with achievement. Mocking or taunting students pushes students away instead of bringing them closer.

Being willing to laugh is an admirable trait in teachers and students alike. That willingness can ease tension and create a better learning environment. Of course, teachers must manage the classroom, but the classroom does not have to be humorless to be manageable. Students do not ignore the upbeat attitudes of their teachers; rather, they are likely to share them. They know when teachers are going the extra mile for them.

Teachers influence student attitudes about school in their classroom management and in their behavior (Hawkins et al., 1999). Attitudes affect teaching philosophies, disciplinary tactics, and intervention strategies. These mind-sets also affect the climate of the school, which tends to mirror the attitudes of teachers and students (Peterson and Skiba, 2001). The school climate, then, is nurtured or neglected by the attitudes of teachers.

Attitudes reflect each other inside and outside of the classroom. Students will frequently embrace the views of the influential adults in their lives. While a confident, authoritative teacher earns the respect of students, a harsh, cynical demeanor breeds resentment. The former supports the educational process; the latter hinders it.

Instilling student happiness does not mean that teachers will make students euphoric about being in a school. Creating student satisfaction, though, requires a level of repose on the teacher's part. It requires neither complacency nor inaction, but rather a sense of well-being that infuses the classroom with pride, warmth, and understanding. Positive attitudes contribute to a better outlook and increased motivation. Demonstrating enthusiasm about learning is contagious.

REINFORCE STRENGTHS

Educators should accentuate adolescent strengths and assets (Lerner and Galambos, 1998). When students know each other's strengths, they become more connected to school (Blum et al., 2002). Highlighting each student's talents increases the potential for every class member to contribute. Students note that teacher favoritism tends to diminish their happiness at being in school. They might think that one group in the class receives preferential treatment.

Preferential treatment cuts away at students' ties to school for those who feel left out. Impartial teaching can be difficult, especially with a group of students with different learning styles, ability levels, and attention spans. Students recognize the teachers who accept every class member, and they are more committed to those classes and more willing to learn.

The use of positive reinforcement seems natural and automatic, but negative behaviors can quickly eclipse the need to keep acknowledging good deeds. Kindergarten students often develop a sense of the kind of students they are, depending on how they are disciplined in the classroom. When the focus is negative, the students often talk only about the bad things that happen in school. They become self-fulfilling prophecies, seeking out the wrong type of attention and taking on a "bad kid" persona.

Similar instances occur in middle school. While it can be very trying for a teacher to detect a student with behavior problems who is doing something positive, until that teacher does, the misbehavior is likely to spiral out of control. Every individual has some good qualities, and when teachers comment on those qualities, they shine even more brightly.

Adolescent group counseling techniques often involve teaching tolerance and empathy. Teachers, naturally, instill these characteristics in their students. Showing teenagers how to be kind, considerate, and tolerant requires modeling on the part of the adults. One does not have to look very far on a school campus to find adults with those qualities.

INTEGRATE CHARACTER EDUCATION

Integrating character education into the instructional process requires very little preparation, yet it yields a great deal. Teachers who connect with students automatically weave character education into the curriculum. They impart values and civic responsibility through their instruction (Peterson and Skiba, 2001). Schools with a strong character education program have fewer disciplinary referrals, fewer fights, and fewer truancy problems (Otten, 2000). These programs teach social competence, tolerance, respect, and values that those students need to lead successful lives.

Tutoring students on appropriate behaviors and cooperation is easily accomplished by scheduling activities throughout the school year. Eleven thousand schools across the country have implemented a character education program called Project Wisdom. As a result, those schools have seen tremendous drops in disciplinary referrals (www.projectwisdom.com). It is one of many fine programs available to schools. Character education links on the Internet are wonderful resources for teachers, counselors, and parents. Such links include www.character.org, www.charactercounts.org, www.giraffe.org, www.actsofkindness.org, and www.dosomething.org.

Through activities that build character, students learn to be considerate as they recognize each other's strengths. To do so, the class members might be asked to give each other a symbolic toast or compliment each classmate verbally or in writing. Additional exercises include classroom discussions on character education words or related quotes.

As the number of small benevolent acts increases, the tone is set for consideration and respect. Asking students to compliment, thank, or help at least one classmate each day fosters altruism throughout the school year. Honest, respectful, and compassionate behaviors are advanced through character education (Peterson and Skiba, 2001). Promoting positive connections between students is a mutually beneficial endeavor.

PROVIDE OPPORTUNITIES FOR SOCIAL INTERACTION

Providing opportunities for social interaction will improve student attitudes and peer relationships. Interaction boosts class participation and achievement. Young people need to socialize. By doing so, they learn how to form healthy relationships. Building social interaction into the instructional process can take the shape of group work, class projects, service learning, or schoolwide activities. Positive peer groups influence the level of school connectedness (Scales, 2000).

Helping students develop healthy peer relationships meets a developmental adolescent need (Blum et al., 2002). Youth have a fundamental need to socialize and develop relationships with their peers. The more isolated teenagers become, the fewer chances they have to sharpen their social skills. On the other hand, students with racially diverse friendship groups are more likely to feel connected to school (Blum et al., 2002). Encouraging interaction and group work in the classroom is one way to help students get to know each other.

Another technique might be to have an advisory class where students engage one another without the pressure to complete assignments or make a grade. Middle school principal Joe Jackson advocates advisory groups, noting that they help students identify with adults who are not evaluating them. Students often view advisory leaders as objective, and may therefore seek advice from those adults.

Cultivating friendships among students does not require the teachers to choose friends for them; rather it requires offering safe opportunities for positive socialization. Teachers must be vigilant about bullying when students interact. Associations with troubled peers might actually encourage drug use and violence as a form of entertainment (Ciampi, 2001). Unfortunately, males are more likely to accept violence as a way to solve a conflict (Bowen and Van Dorn, 2002).

Victimized students are not difficult to spot, even though they may not have revealed their negative experiences to their teachers. Victims rarely feel safe or happy at school. While bullies usually have a small following, victims will withdraw rather than associate with others (Nansel et al., 2001). Along with preventing bullying, teaching tolerance, assertiveness, problem-solving, and decision-making skills will aid students in developing sound friendships.

Research indicates, though, that risk factors increase for students with attachments to peers who do use drugs and alcohol (Substance Abuse, 2002). The earlier the use of illicit drugs, the higher the risk for deviant behaviors (Barnes, Welte, and Hoffman, 2002; Brook and Balka, 1999). Drug use or deviant behavior has detrimental effects on learning and interferes with school bonding. In the midst of directing young people toward good relationships and high academic standards, the attitude toward student commitment is crucial.

ADVOCATE FOR STUDENTS

All educators must advocate for students. Students require continual support and advocacy. Teachers and parents are the biggest advocates for children, yet sometimes the recipients are not aware of the huge amount of positive support behind them. Many adults spend countless hours searching out the best books, better learning conditions, improved teaching tools, all in an effort to reach and teach students in the best possible way. They are continually trying to find better ways to meet the needs of students.

Advocacy should not be confused with leniency, especially when it comes to students who break the rules. Prescribing fair treatment for all students is one way of advocating for them. Overindulgence or refusing to believe that a child has misbehaved can be a grave error. Student satisfaction is not overlooked when setting limits, imposing discipline, and building support for the educational process. When students feel accepted in the classroom, roadblocks to learning are removed. As their sense of well-being increases, students are more apt to commit to school and look forward to continuing their education.

School connectedness intensifies when students are content at school. Passing judgment on students, being distrustful of them, or treating them unfairly, prevents students from connecting to school. Just as happiness is essential in building connectedness, so is a sense of fairness. That sense of justice increases when young people recognize that school disciplinary policies are based on unbiased rules.

Students need to know about the efforts that the adults make on their behalf. Young people can be given a say in some of the decisions that affect them. They can learn to advocate for themselves and gain an appreciation of the strong support behind them. That knowledge builds confidence, trust, and establishes the sense of fairness that they need if they are to have strong ties to school.

CHAPTER 5

Fairness

The Teachers at This School Treat Students Fairly

Fairness is extremely important to adolescents. As they begin to question authority and make their own decisions, teens need to be convinced that they are being treated fairly. Fairness and justice are also equally important values to adults. In dealing with young people, though, those standards are often dismissed by parents, teachers, and other adults. It often becomes all about proving who is in control and making sure it is not the students. Tolerance, justice, and open-mindedness are occasionally replaced by hypocrisy and vindictiveness.

As youth form their own ethics and principles, their sense of justice intensifies. Just as adults do, young people know when rules are enforced impartially. Students can also readily pinpoint disparities. Deceptive and unfair practices antagonize young people, pushing them further away from the educational environment and the critical connections they need. Victims are less likely to perceive being treated fairly at school when there is an ongoing pattern of bullying by students or teachers.

Unduly harsh or hostile responses from adults discourage students from learning and connecting. Consistent disciplinary policies reduce the likelihood of those types of adult reactions. Overly punitive measures tend to weaken school ties. Perceptions about school cohesion and safety also decline in a harsh or rigid environment (Mulvey and Cauffman, 2001). Using coercive tactics or draconian regulations to control student behavior actually backfires (Price et al., 2002). When students begin to feel oppressed or persecuted, their commitment to school wanes.

Fair, rather than excessively rigid, disciplinary practices produce greater student commitment in school. Equitable procedures effectively deal with misbehavior and bullying as well (Smith et al., 1999). Grossly punitive policies have the potential to escalate school violence rather than curb it. An inherent danger exists with the use of punitive action without taking a comprehensive, schoolwide approach to address the problem of school violence fairly.

While harsh school conditions can exacerbate bullying behaviors and student misconduct, equitable practices reduce or prevent the behaviors from occurring (Olweus, 1993). Olweus, a leading researcher in the problem of bullying, describes the conditions that educators need to create in order to promote fairness, safety, and prevention of bullying. The emphasis is placed on changing the school's ecology (Greenberg, Domitrovich, and Bumbarger, 1999). The ecological focus of the Olweus Bullying Prevention Program approach is associated with higher school connectedness. Environmental changes can transform the school climate and student outlook.

When schools provide a safe, warm, and nurturing environment, behavioral problems often decrease (Harris et al., 2002). Several steps can be taken to make sure that students feel they are treated fairly. Some involve whole school approaches, while others deal with classroom management. Again, these simple measures are routine in schools that are committed to connecting with students.

UNDERSTAND ADOLESCENT DEVELOPMENT

Understanding adolescent development will increase levels of school connectedness. Adolescents are not likely to connect in schools that fail to meet their developmental needs (Blum et al., 2002). In order to optimize the potential for learning, the educational environment must fit adolescent needs. Understanding adolescents can prove invaluable when communicating with young people. During adolescence, young people are undergoing rapid physical, cognitive, and psychosocial changes (Karcher and Lee, 2002).

Physical changes can be dramatic for adolescents as they begin to resemble adults in features, shape, and size. With these changes, young people often become overly self-conscious. In addition, they may feel awkward and clumsy as their bodies mature. As they develop physically, adolescents also begin to form their own identities and think about their sexuality.

From changes in their appearance and the new interest in forming close relationships with others, the brain also continues to change during the teen years (Spinks, 2002). Adolescent development has been dubbed a period of "exploration and experimentation" (Lerner and Galambos, 1998). As they explore and experiment, teen interests and activities leave lasting imprints upon the brain. Their negative behaviors actually compromise neurological growth and functioning. During this maturation process, adolescents develop reasoning skills, judgment, and impulse control (Spinks, 2002). In addition, teens become much more efficient at processing information (Lerner and Galambos).

While the prefrontal cortex matures and higher order thinking skills evolve, teen behavior appears to be spontaneous, emotional, and impulsive, and controlled by the amygdala (Cooke). Eventually, judgment skills improve and impulsivity decreases, but adolescent brains are malleable and exposure to stress interferes with the healthy changes in brain chemistry and development (Landau, 2001). Important neurological connections may become lost or damaged due to repeated abuse and social stressors (Lepore and Bobinchock, 2003).

The threat to healthy adolescent development is real. In 1998, 50 percent of the approximately 28 million adolescents in this country engaged in two or more risky behaviors within that year. The risky behaviors included smoking, alcohol use, or drug use; sexual activity (unprotected sex, teen pregnancy); dropping out; and delinquency (criminal and violent offenses) (Lerner and Galambos, 1998). As young people explore their newfound freedoms and responsibilities, they are more likely to engage in risk-taking behaviors.

While some unhealthy behaviors are regarded as normal teenage experiences, the age and frequency of the exposure raise the potential for more dangerous behaviors. By the time they are seniors, the majority of students (80 percent) have tried alcohol. Over half (51 percent) of eighth-graders also admit to having tried alcohol (Eaton et al., 2004). The earlier an adolescent is introduced to unhealthy behaviors, the more serious those acts become. For instance, alcohol-related problems during adolescence are also associated with other negative or antisocial practices (Why do some people drink too much, 2000).

Adult guidance and support are vital during the teen years. Healthy development depends on the relationships that adolescents forge with family members and other adults. McNeely et al. (2002) note that adolescents need opportunities to increase their independent functioning and competence. They also need to socialize, to arrive at their own opinions, and to question authority (Jaffe, 1998). As they endeavor to become more self-reliant, adolescents begin to challenge decisions made by adults inside and outside of the classroom.

MANAGE CLASSROOM BEHAVIOR

A well-managed classroom is the bedrock of school connectedness. Maintaining a structured classroom, though, requires organization and forethought. The benefits, however, are enormous. The organization of the class will allow the students to know what to expect as soon as they walk through the door. More importantly, students will know the rules regarding performance, behavioral standards, and high expectations for achievement. A structured management plan allows students to feel secure within the classroom.

A well-managed classroom offers a balanced, comfortable learning environment. Well-managed classrooms have the same common denominators: clear guidelines for behavior and work, student involvement, and acceptance (Blum et al., 2002). Of course, the sooner students experience instruction in well-managed classrooms, the better the outcome. Research points out that well-managed elementary school classrooms lower the level of aggression in middle school (Kellam, 2002).

Student attitudes improve in a well-managed classroom (Hawkins et al., 1999). Classroom management skills also reduce educators' job stress and enhance teacher performance (Kellam, 2002). Awareness of class rules, expectations, and beliefs also helps students adhere to classroom guidelines. Class beliefs and expectations also affect aggressive and violent behaviors (Anderson et al., 2001). When the classroom norms include social responsibility, students adopt similar attitudes

(Henry et al., 2000). Consistent behavioral feedback will also bolster commitment in the classroom. That commitment reinforces trust among students and teachers.

Students should be included in the making of classroom rules and policies. Their participation increases their sense of responsibility and accountability. It also helps students refine their self-monitoring skills. Students do not have to make all the rules. They are more likely, though, to adhere to rules in which they have had a say. Classrooms that promote self-discipline aid in building strong ties to students. In addition, those classes will have fewer disciplinary referrals (Kellam, 2002).

Having student input and clearly informing students about decisions that affect them leaves no room for misunderstanding. Students are capable of accepting the consequences of their own poor choices and to not blame anyone else. When students contribute to the management of the classroom, they feel more connected to school. Student input on class rules, grading criteria, and the management of the classroom increases their autonomy and self-control (Blum et al., 2002).

As classroom management declines, so does school connectedness (Kellam, 2002). Being respectful preserves student dignity; treating them with disrespect takes it away. Teaching should not involve belittling, degrading, or humiliating students, especially not in front of their peers. Embarrassing students does not promote learning; instead, it creates animosity. Talking down to students only leaves the students angry, not thinking about the behaviors that need to be changed.

In his book, *The Shame Response to Rejection,* Dr. Herbert Thomas (1997) notes that individual responses to shame vary, but often include intense physical anguish. In addition, he advises teachers not to use their authority to inflict insults and injury upon students. Shaming students is neither productive nor conducive to learning. Constructive criticism, rather than harsh rebukes, yields far better academic and behavioral results.

Challenges to authority can often lead to power struggles if the adults allow them to go too far. Giving the young person latitude does not mean that teachers have to relinquish their authority. Limits can still be defined and young people need to know when they have crossed the limit of acceptable behavior.

Consistency permits students to know exactly what to expect on the school grounds. It should also follow students into the classroom. Consistency lends itself to clarity and understanding. If the guidelines are unclear, then the students may push the limits. Students are often taken aback when they are disciplined for not following unclear rules. Everyone likes to know what to expect; uncertainty leads to confusion and a degree of unfairness that is unlikely to go away.

The American Federation of Teachers (2000) cited consistency as an integral component of fair disciplinary codes. Student behaviors can only be addressed effectively when rules are administered evenhandedly and appropriately. Consistency does not curtail a teacher's ability to be flexible; rather, it allows the consideration of alternative approaches. It also provides a foundation for cohesion among students. When teachers consistently address problem behaviors, student conduct often improves (Henry et al., 2000). Students are given a sense of predictability when teachers are consistent. Being consistent also generates student compliance; arbitrary rules and expectations produce dissension.

Using humor to defuse potential discipline problems can help. Rather than allowing a situation to escalate, finding the humor in it will help the student admit to and stop unacceptable behaviors. Humor is also a recommended strategy in dealing with bullies. Of course, it does not apply when the bullying has turned dangerous, but levity can prevent the situation from getting that far.

Situations that escalate might be tempered with kindness and humor. Teaching students how to own a problem humorously can constitute a valuable coping strategy. Humor helps reduce tension and is an important part of developing a relationship with young people. Adolescents often go through emotional difficulties with their friends and families. How adults interact with them helps them deal effectively with their problems. In addition, positive student-teacher interactions help build confidence and improve commitment to school.

ESTABLISH TRUST

Establishing trust necessitates imparting some key values. First, honesty is non-negotiable. Everyone knows that honesty is the best policy.

Honesty is a principal concern for adolescents. In order to develop a trusting relationship with an adult, young people must be certain that the adult is trustworthy. Students know when someone is lying to them. They also seem to know when an adult has no intention of following through with a promise. Reliability is a chief component in a trusting relationship. Adolescents want their teachers to do what they say they will do, or explain why.

Forming a trusting relationship with students is paramount in building school connectedness. One way to develop such a relationship is encouraging student self-management (McNeely et al., 2002). Giving young people the opportunity to monitor themselves builds competence. When students participate in the decision-making process, they assume more responsibility in the life of the classroom. In addition, the atmosphere within the classroom improves along with the higher level of trust given to the students.

Counselors must explain that when a student or client is a danger to himself or others, certain information cannot remain confidential. Taking the student through the steps of what will happen if such a disclosure is made increases the level of trust. Helping students to be honest themselves requires honesty on the part of the adults.

Candor builds trust and a sense of fairness among students. Truthfulness promotes loyalty and respect. Students emulate the dependability and reliability of their teachers. They appreciate their impartiality and sincerity in attempting to treat everyone fairly. In addition, students are more likely to adhere to class rules when the integrity of the teacher is not in question.

Openness is also an effective way to reach parents. Such frankness increases parental support and, in turn, improves teacher effectiveness. Straightforward discussions with parents can lead to a better understanding of student behavior. Parent and teacher communications can be invaluable to students. When adolescents see the adults in their lives working together, they are more likely to commit to school and to change problem behaviors.

Admitting mistakes is a key aspect of developing trust. Admitting a mistake is not always easy. I believe that parents and educators always want to be right. After all, they are to be looked up to, not down on. Holding a position of authority, though, does not remove the fallibility of being human. One of my posters reads, "The only mistake is one that we do not learn from." Mistakes can be excellent lessons in humility and success.

One principal with whom I have had the pleasure to work has earned his staff's respect through his leadership skills and through his mistakes. When he has erred, he learns from it and teaches others about it. He openly discusses the actions that he needs to change in dealing with a particular situation. His honesty allows his staff to see him as a real person, not as infallible. This kind of candor also gives teachers the chance to reflect on their own responses.

When teachers admit their mistakes, students see them as real people. Teachers who are not afraid to admit their own frailties help students forgive their own shortcomings. Students respect a teacher even more when that teacher is not afraid of students seeing his or her mistakes or weaknesses.

Respecting students is vital to the establishment of trust. Ideally, the classroom should be characterized by mutual respect. This is not always the case, but good teachers communicate respect to their students and receive it in return. That respect fosters a sense of fairness that students need in order to connect in school. According to a survey of 123 future principals, treating students equally and fairly was essential (Harris and Lowery, 2002).

Educators must offer students the same respect in order to maintain fairness within the classroom and on the school campus. Students deserve to be treated fairly regardless of who their parents are, what their socioeconomic status is, and regardless of race and gender. Respect preserves the dignity of the students. When students are underestimated or devalued, they feel unfairly singled out.

One principal noted that forcing a student to do something is not as effective as encouragement. He confided that force does not equate to learning, an old assumption that is often difficult to overcome. Some teachers still believe that students have to be afraid of authority figures in order to learn from them. In fact, quite the opposite is true. Students withdraw from the learning environment if they do not feel safe. In addition, teacher indifference diminishes a teen's self-respect. Respect, however, signals approval and is prized by the students. It is also indicative of stability within the classroom and on the school campus.

CULTIVATE LIFE SKILLS

Cultivating life skills will help students' sense of fairness grow. Life skills are those abilities that will help adolescents successfully navigate the path to adulthood. Young people go from having a childish innocence to developing their own ideals and values. Helping students adopt values that include understanding, compassion, and concern for others will build resilience and fortify school bonds.

Fostering life skills involves teaching students how to make wise decisions, communicate effectively, and accept one another (Junge, Manglallan, and Raskauskas, 2003). Students should be encouraged to discuss ways of addressing the problems they encounter. As students gain mastery in these areas, their scholastic achievement and peer relationships will improve. Students learn valuable life skills from their teachers on a daily basis. They learn coping and problem-solving skills that will benefit them for the rest of their lives. In addition, they become more capable of controlling their emotions.

MODEL SELF-CONTROL

Self-control is a pivotal factor in classroom management. It is also a key to helping students control themselves. It is not always easy to quell emotions, especially in the heat of an argument or when trying to regain the attention of a classroom of students. If a teacher has an emotional outburst, though, students will focus on the teacher's reactions rather than their own behaviors. Keeping the anger (or sadness) in check will help keep student conduct the focal point and become the impetus for changing unacceptable behaviors.

Teachers are not expected to be impassive in front of their students. They should, however, avoid acting in a way that would breed resentment and animosity. An antagonistic or hostile teacher has no place in the classroom. Dealing with student misbehaviors can certainly be frustrating, but meting out disciplinary practices as dispassionately as possible can be more effective than yelling at or arguing with the student.

If the classroom is a scene of constant turmoil, students can become fearful and apprehensive as soon as they step through the door. Anxiety, fear, and stress create a difficult learning environment. Shidler

(2001) notes that aggressive teachers endorse violence through their own conduct. The author further notes that teachers who behave in a hostile manner toward students might be more likely to ignore bullying (Shidler).

In their study of the social context for bullying behaviors, Espelage, Bosworth, and Simon (2000) also warned that students learn to engage in violent behaviors from adults and peers. The same social environment, however, can promote prosocial behaviors and positive methods of achieving goals. When teachers and students refuse to tolerate disruptive behaviors, aggression is lowered (Henry et al., 2000). Preventing violence, then, requires teachers to model amicable actions, cooperation, and problem solving. Solving problems in a nonconfrontational manner shows students how to settle their own conflicts peacefully (Peterson and Skiba, 2001).

Monitoring student behavior in the classroom and on the school grounds is a huge responsibility. Couple it with actually educating the children and the role of the teacher can be a weighty one indeed. Not only do teachers have to ensure that their daily lesson plans meet local, state, and national standards, but these professionals are also trying to make sure that students feel connected to school. In doing so, educators establish a sense of fairness among the young people. That sense of fairness promotes security on the school grounds and keeps students safe.

CHAPTER 6

Safety
I Feel Safe in This School

Safety is a primary concern for schools across this country and around the world. Terrorism has intensified the need for safety precautions at schools, airports, and other places that draw large numbers of people. Threats to children's safety are real and dangerous. Within the school walls, bullying threatens student safety (Garbarino and de Lara, 2002). It is the most frequent type of victimization at school (Flannery and Singer, 1999). Almost five million students are bullied in schools each year (Harris et al., 2002). Aggressive and bullying behaviors often begin during the elementary school years, but become increasingly more harmful, frightening, and intense during adolescence (Bracher, 2000).

Fear of bullying contributes to the absences of 160,000 children from school per day (Colvin et al., 1998). Threats or fear of being attacked also leads to weapon carrying in schools (DuRant et al., 1997). In 1998, an estimated 100,000 children carried weapons to school to protect themselves from bullies (Colvin et al., 1998). Chronic bullying precipitated more than two thirds of the school shootings in this country (Harris et al., 2002). Although bullying does not often escalate into gun violence, the availability of weapons greatly increases that potential (Hill and Drolet, 1999).

Victimization and bullying are both linked to weapon carrying, fighting, and injuries at school (Nansel et al., 2003). While several factors interfere with students' sense of safety at school, bullying is the most insidious. Victims become anxious, isolated from their friends, and are likely to experience psychosomatic symptoms (Voors, 2000; Flannery and Singer, 1999). Bystanders experience trauma from just viewing acts of aggression (Garbarino and de Lara, 2002). Witnessing violence is also predictive of fighting injuries for both boys and girls (Borowsky and Ireland, 2004). Direct or indirect victimization leads to social alienation, anxiety, and depression (Voors, 2000; Flannery and Singer, 1999). Depression is linked to future fight-related injuries, especially among girls (Borowsky and Ireland, 2004). Altogether, victimization interferes with the learning process, as victims find it impossible to concentrate.

School connectedness, however, was found to reduce the likelihood of students bringing weapons to school (Kodjo, Auinger, and Ryan, 2003). When students, especially adolescent males, have a strong affiliation with school, they are more likely to feel safe there. The more connected students are to school, the less likelihood of bullying being a serious problem.

The perception of limited safety in an educational environment often reflects levels of dangerous behaviors in school (Bowen and Van Dorn, 2002). Bullying, weapon carrying, alcohol use, and availability of drugs hinder school safety and school connectedness. Students who feel unsafe in school often have truancy problems, poor grades, and participate in at-risk behaviors. Bowen and Van Dorn (2002) note that the educational opportunities for all students suffer when students feel vulnerable.

Schools must address these fears by preventing violence before it erupts. Students who do not feel safe are more likely to feel estranged from teachers, peers, and from the educational experience. They are more likely to engage in smoking, alcohol and drug use, truancy, early sexual activity, and bullying (Bonny et al., 2000; Natvig et al., 2001; Ellickson and McGuigan, 2000; Natvig et al., 2001).

Bullying involvement through victimization and perpetration poses the gravest danger for the aggressors themselves (Nansel et al., 2003). Victims who become aggressive are more likely to retaliate violently. Kaltiala-Heino and colleagues (2000) note that victims who become violent themselves are also at the highest risk for alcohol and substance abuse problems. Kumpulainen, Rasanen, and Puura (2001) determine that combative or aggressive victims are also at greatest risk for psychiatric disorders and suicidal ideation. Victim aggressors are more likely to have attention-deficit disorders, oppositional defiant disorders, depression, and other conduct disorders (Kumpulainen, Rasanen, and Puura, 2001; Tani, Greenman, Schneider, and Fregoso, 2003; Unnever and Cornell, 2003; Van der Wal, de Wit, and Hirasing, 2003).

Schools are the primary sources for effective prevention of aggressive behaviors. Even if parents reinforce aggression at home, schools have the opportunity to create conditions that reduce those behaviors (McEvoy and Welker, 2000). Schools are important determinants of bullying behaviors, especially for adolescents (Espelage et al., 2000). Schools that provide a safe learning environment also promote, model, and shape pro-social behaviors (Khosropour and Walsh, 2001). Below are some safety strategies.

KEEP SCHOOLS SMALL

Keeping schools small may be financially impossible for some systems, but the benefits can far outweigh the costs. Students feel more connected to school when attending small rather than large schools. Teachers are more apt to develop close relationships with students in smaller schools. Large schools preclude the opportunity for teachers to interact with all the young people on the campus.

Garbarino and de Lara (2002) note school size is a critical issue affecting student safety. The researchers point out that school populations with more than five hundred students tend to be more unpredictable and difficult to supervise (Winter, 2001). High schools with six hundred to twelve hundred students, though, may provide the best opportunity for academic achievement, while those with fewer than three hundred students are not ideal for learning.

Large student populations can also be more complicated to supervise (Garbarino and deLara, 2002). Students inherently know the dangers of a campus that is too large. As school size increases, connections between students and teachers decrease (McNeely et al., 2002). Those campuses may have a high level of bullying, smoking, drugs, and weapon carrying. As school size increases, the level of criminal activity at school may also rise.

Many types of crime occur on middle and high school campuses: harassment, extortion, robbery, and assault. The National Crime Victimization Survey revealed that some 2.7 million crimes involving violence occur on or around a school campus (Hill and Drolet, 1999). One in six middle to high school students reported being victims of violent offenses while at school (Bowen and Van Dorn, 2002). Even though teachers have no control over school size, their consistent input, advocacy, and vigilance can keep children safe.

Although Olweus (1993) notes that school size is not a factor in determining bullying, the potential for aggressive behaviors increases when supervision is limited. Students need to know that the adults employed by the school are supervising the campus during unstructured activities, i.e. lunch, changing classes, bathrooms, hallways, corridors, and the school grounds after school. Adult awareness of problem areas increases student safety and the sense of security.

In addition, small schools tend to have lower dropout rates. Fewer students drop out of schools with low enrollment numbers and fewer school changes between grades (Alspaugh, 1998). As school transitions increase, attendance, motivation, and school connectedness decline. The campus atmosphere is just as important as the climate within the classroom.

CREATE A POSITIVE SCHOOL CLIMATE

A healthy school climate is the single most important element of school connectedness (Blum et al., 2002). A positive school climate should be reflected in the attitudes of the faculty and staff. The school climate is also reflected in school and classroom maintenance, policy enforcement, and student-teacher interaction (Holtappels and Meier, 2000). The potential for violence and aggression is influenced by the school climate. The educational environment sets the standards for behavior, thereby fostering or restricting school connectedness. If the environment makes unrealistic expectations of the students, the climate promotes problems rather than deters them (Holtappels and Meier, 2000).

Olweus (2003) supports the need for a warm, positive social climate that is conducive to student involvement and strong relationships. The school climate must help students feel safe enough to trust the adults and to learn. Educators must be able to recognize the important social function of a positive school climate. An oppressive climate produces negative interaction between the students and teachers (Holtappels and Meier, 2000).

Students should feel confident enough to trust any adult on the school campus. Positive connections are not restricted to teachers; counselors, administrators, and support personnel can transform children's lives. Every adult on the school grounds has the opportunity to connect with young people on a daily basis.

Relationships between teachers and staff members also play an important role in the school climate (Kallestad, Olweus, and Alsaker, 1998). Students can sense tension among adults whether at home or in school. When teachers do not respect each other, school commitment falters. Collegial relationships, flexibility, and teacher leadership skills also affect the educational environment. Modeling pro-social relationships must begin with the adults at the helm of the school.

Educators can also address the environmental factors within the school that impact bullying. Promoting pro-social attitudes, behaviors, and classroom routines will inhibit bullying and reduce the likelihood of school violence (Olweus, 2003). In the United States, the proportion of school shootings involving multiple victims increased from zero percent in 1992 to 42 percent in 1999 (Anderson et al., 2001). The students who carried out school homicides were more than twice as likely to have been bullied than their victims or peers were. In addition, more than half of the perpetrators gave some warning of the impending violence. Recommendations for prevention must also include heeding and responding to such signs.

INCREASE ADULT SUPERVISION

Most school principals agree that adults on campus must be visible and present wherever students are—in the hallways, bathrooms, cafeteria, locker rooms, and throughout the day. The adult presence is one of the most valuable environmental prevention tools that schools can use (Hoang, 2001). Handbooks, codes of conduct, and safety plans also provide guidelines to increase safety and handle crises.

Educators must be attentive to the specific needs of their students. Adolescents need to have developmentally appropriate levels of supervision. Meeting this need requires adults to remain alert while giving adolescents room to interact with one another. Too much freedom or inadequate supervision might open the door for inappropriate behaviors, while too many restrictions might give students the sense that they are not trusted. Being aware of the changes in attitudes, behaviors, and movements of adolescents on a school campus makes schools safer.

Teachers must be alert to threats and take them seriously. The seriousness of making threats should be communicated to students. Teens must believe that they have an interest in helping to make their school safe and be instructed to report all threats, even when they think that the person issuing the threat is "just kidding." Allowing students to report concerns anonymously may convey the value of reporting. All staff members should know the process for reporting threats and dealing with other serious offenses.

Staying alert also requires knowing what to do in the event of an emergency. A thorough knowledge of the school safety plan is instrumental in dealing calmly with crises. Knowing how to respond to a particular crisis saves time, if not lives. The plan must be implemented as soon as an incident occurs, so reviewing the process at the beginning of each school year can help keep teachers and students safe. Regular drills also give students and staff members an opportunity to practice the necessary procedures for lockdowns, severe weather, fire, and other emergencies.

Students admit to feeling safer when they have regularly participated in drills at school. The teens develop a sense of security and assuage their own fears with their knowledge of what to do when a catastrophic event happens at school. The young people trust in the adults around them to know and follow the safety plan. The presence of adults in critical areas around the school helps ensure safety at all times.

ENLIST COMMUNITY SUPPORT

Enlisting community support will assist schools in connecting with students. Religious groups, nonprofit agencies, and local businesses support schools in the form of tutoring, funding, and other services. Among the strategies recommended in the wake of the Columbine shootings, the director of the National School Safety Center advised schools to develop a close relationship with law enforcement (Stephens, 1999). The presence of police officers or security guards after school activities such as football games also reduces the incidence of violence and other at-risk behaviors (Bowen and Van Dorn, 2002). In addition, school resource officers provide an invaluable resource to schools.

These officers create a positive attitude toward law enforcement among students. The collaboration between law enforcement and schools has helped to reduce the level of violence on campuses (Bowman, 2002). This is especially important since some statistics indicated that a violent incident was occurring on a school campus as often as every six seconds (Grant et al., 1998). Violent offenses often begin with some form of bullying.

PREVENT BULLYING

Bullying compromises student safety and creates a hostile learning environment. Schools must set the tone in bullying prevention with clear rules, expectations, and adequate supervision. A structured bullying prevention program is not always necessary. Teachers, though, must be able to recognize when bullying is occurring and intervene (Eckman, 2001). Bullying should not be condoned or tolerated. Not accepting bullying behaviors does not equate to a zero tolerance policy; alone, such policies have not been effective in bullying prevention (Eckman, 2001).

Prevention policies should involve guidelines to deal with victims, aggressive victims, bullies, and witnesses (Harris et al., 2002). Most students have been directly or indirectly affected by bullying. All students should be involved in prevention efforts. In deterring bullying, students must be equipped with strategies to deal with aggressive behaviors. The tendency is often to fight fire with fire, and to respond to violence with more violence. Retaliation is a common response that is often encouraged at home. Such behaviors actually tend to increase for boys; as they get older, twelve-year-old boys were more than 2.7 times as likely to hit back than eleven-year-olds were. (Price et al., 2002).

Male students with poor grades are also more likely to retaliate (Price et al., 2002). Parents and students often justify striking back as self-defense. The parents frequently hold outdated attitudes that view hitting as an acceptable response to aggression, as long as their child was not the one who started the fight. These responses often escalate rather than reduce the level of violence. Other antiquated ideas fuel bullying and coercive behavior rather than contain the violence. Parents and teachers frequently have views that perpetuate aggression. Teachers might hold the view that students need to learn to solve their problems on their own (Colvin et al., 1998).

Teaching critical problem-solving, coping, and anger management skills provides useful ways for students to interact with their peers. Such instruction is a decisive factor in violence prevention programs (Cooper, Lutenbacher, and Faccia, 2000). Peer mediation programs also promote a positive school climate and healthy relationships within the school (Lane-Garon, 2000). While students benefit from learning and using conflict resolution skills, such training by itself will not deter bullying (Colvin et al., 1998). Sometimes teachers will minimize the problem or think that they lack support when confronting a refractory student. Adults may even fear the bully themselves, especially if they have been victimized (Colvin et al., 1998). The failure to address bullying behaviors, however, will aggravate the problem. When students do not feel safe in school, they sometimes seek to protect themselves in dangerous ways.

The potential for weapon carrying increases as aggressive or victimized children grow older. Eleven-year olds were more likely to carry a weapon to school than their younger counterparts were (Price et al., 2002). In a North Carolina study of 2,227 middle school students, 17 percent had carried a weapon to school. Among that percentage, 14 percent of the students had brought knives, while the remaining 3 percent had carried a gun into the school for protection (DuRant et al., 1999). Statistics differ each year in the actual number of weapons brought onto school campuses, with some figures are as high as 250,000 (Dwyer, 1999). Risk factors for weapon carrying include tobacco, alcohol, or drug use, along with being an older male (DuRant et al., 1999).

When teachers fail to step in and take action against bullying, bullies, victims, and bystanders take this as tacit approval (Eckman, 2001). Some adults might even deliberately look the other way when a provocative or an unpopular victim is brutalized. The justification might be that the student was "asking for it" (Colvin et al., 1998). The messages that adults send about bullying, fighting, and discipline influence bullying behaviors (Espelage, Bosworth, and Simon, 2000). These messages must be clear: no student deserves to be bullied.

In order to prevent bullying, Colvin and colleagues (1998) recommend that educators seek out research-based programs with valid behavioral standards. In addition, the researchers note that one component of the program should involve social skills training to replace bullying and antisocial behaviors (Colvin et al., 1998). Initially, though, schools must first determine the scope of the problem.

After they know the magnitude of the problem, schools can discuss the direction of their program. Administrators must decide whether to focus on school connectedness, or to investigate bullying further with instruments such as the Revised Olweus Bully Victim Questionnaire. In addition, schools may choose to implement a bully prevention program and assess both areas with pre- and post-tests to determine the effectiveness of the prevention program in building school connectedness.

Schools may elect to use the School Connectedness Scale first to identify the level of school connectedness. Schools with high levels of connectedness do not endorse violence in any form, including bullying. If the school connectedness scores are low, more information about the bullying problem should be gathered. Tools to measure the extent of bullying can vary in price, from free bullying surveys on the Internet to research-based tools such as the Revised Olweus Bully Victim Questionnaire. The public health cost linked to bullying and low school connectedness justifies the need to single out the most appropriate avenue for intervention (Centers for Disease Control, 2002; Hawkins et al., 1999). Problems related to bullying and weak school ties have adverse consequences that shadow individuals into adulthood.

Prevention strategies should focus on specific at-risk groups, or universal designs that benefit the entire population. Either way, schools should have well-defined programs to prevent bullying (Hoang, 2001). Programs that target high-risk groups are moderately successful in reducing aggressive behaviors (Mytton, DiGuiseppi, Gough, Taylor, and Logan, 2002). Schoolwide, or universal programs, however, may yield the most effectiveness in reducing and preventing school violence (Mytton, et al., 2002). Some of the categories of universal strategies include violence prevention, social and cognitive skills training, multi-dimensional components, and ecological programs (Greenberg et al., 1999).

Curriculum-based programs provide training in peer mentoring, mediation, and other conflict resolution skills for students (Hoang, 2001). This training provides students with useful skills to deal with conflicts peacefully. In addition, young people learn strategies that help them increase school safety. Adolescents themselves become more informed about warning signs of violence and how to prevent incidents from occurring.

With training, students learn how to prevent bullying instead of passively supporting aggression as a witness or bystander. In addition, students need avenues to report incidents of violence without fear of retaliation. Many of the school shooters shared their violent plans with classmates, yet none took their threats seriously (Willert, 2002). Many young people often succumb to pressure not to tell adults (Lamberg, 1998).

Students must feel comfortable enough in school to report incidents of violence, weapon carrying, and other dangerous behaviors (Willert, 2002). In addition, young people must also have a sense of responsibility and commitment to school. They must want to take part in keeping their school safe (Lamberg, 1998). Students involved in violent behaviors have weak ties to school and no sense of belonging (Willert, 2002). Aggressive students may view the school climate as oppressive or stifling.

Burns, Andrews, and Szabo (2002) note that programs that improve the school environment also improve students' behavior and sense of well-being. The Olweus Bullying Prevention Program is one program that focuses on environmental changes. The prevention program emphasizes changing conditions within the school setting (Greenberg et al., 1999). Stoolmiller, Eddy, and Reid (2000) determined that aggressive behaviors in schools were effectively reduced through whole school approaches. One such program is the Olweus Bully Prevention Program that yielded significant reductions in reports of bullying behaviors and improvements within the school environment itself (Greenberg et al., 1999).

The plan developed by Olweus is one of the most effective of its kind (Nansel et al., 2003). The program has been implemented in many countries, including the United States. Although some indicators of school connectedness have not been associated with bullying, the components of the Olweus program correlate with all aspects of school connectedness. The program addresses school safety in the classroom and throughout the entire school (Olweus, 1993).

The Revised Olweus Bully Victim Questionnaire helps educators to identify the extent of the problem and to direct increased supervision to "hot spots" that bullies frequent (Olweus, 1993). It can be an important aspect of the overall prevention program. Administering a questionnaire to determine the extent of the bullying problem within the school is vital in an effective bullying prevention program. Such a measure generates awareness of the problem and acts as a springboard for subsequent interventions.

Survey results should be shared with students, parents, and faculty to ensure commitment to form a prevention plan. Additional training materials should prepare the adults to target the problem. Classroom and school policies must reflect consistent disciplinary policies to thwart bullying. Although individual interventions are recommended, the primary focus of prevention with the Olweus program involves changes within the school environment (Olweus, 1993). Colvin and his colleagues (1998) recommend that educators also take a proactive rather than a reactive stance to bullying by promoting prosocial behaviors throughout the school.

A wide variety of bullying questionnaires and prevention programs is available for educators. Programs differ in range and design, but have similar objectives. A curriculum has also been developed in an effort to reduce bullying and improve school safety. In 2000, the U.S. Surgeon General proposed that schools employ research-based methods to address the problem of school violence (U.S. Department of Health and Human Services, 2000). The Center for the Study and Prevention of Violence cites several successful models for violence prevention, including the Olweus program (Olweus, 1999). The goal is to identify the extent of the problem and to implement a comprehensive plan based on the needs of the students.

Making the school a fortress will not necessarily increase school safety. For instance, the presence of metal detectors was not found to increase students' sense of security (Mulvey and Cauffman, 2001). Nonetheless, school districts have quickly become the largest purchasers of metal detectors (Hill and Drolet, 1999). Security measures, though, should increase safety without hindering learning (Hoang, 2001). Improving supervision and awareness of the problem increases school safety by reducing the incidence of victimization and bullying (Olweus, 1993).

Additionally, more qualitative research into the area of victimization and bullying would provide greater insight into the types of bullying that occur most frequently. Kimmel and Mahler (2003) note that school shooters experienced an inordinate amount of harassment about their sexual orientation. Accusations of being homosexual were directed against some of the students who became school shooters. Sexual taunts deny students equal access to education, thereby presenting serious obstacles to learning and social functioning (Pelligrini, 2002). In order to overcome sexual bullying, educators must involve parents and enforce sanctions that include sexual harassment as a form of violence (Levin-Epstein, 2003).

CHAPTER 7

Hope for the Future

Inspiration for the future can be found on school campuses everywhere. Most young people are eager to lead the way to tomorrow. School connections will ensure that their path is safe. As school ties are strengthened, school connectedness can be the conduit for a brighter future. School connectedness, however, depends upon many variables. It involves caring teachers in socially integrated, well-managed classrooms in schools that are not too large (Blum et al., 2002).

At least once a week, a very caring teacher will comment to me that a student has no hope of graduating and leading a productive life. The teacher will deplore the student's upbringing, desperate home life and circumstances, and insist that the student has too many strikes against him or her. When I suggest that the value of school connections should not be discounted, the teacher will shake her head in disbelief and ask if I really believe that. My reply is "absolutely."

I also know firsthand of the important role that school connectedness played in my upbringing. My mother took her own life when I was only eight years old. From that point on, school filled a void in my life. School gave me a place to belong, a place where I felt safe and happy. Many teachers took me under their wings to try to shield me against the insurmountable odds that I myself faced. Other factors certainly influenced my life's course, but school connections kept me steered in the right direction.

Of course, the sooner the connection is made, the better chance there is of safeguarding a student from risky behaviors. Adolescence, though, has its own perils and that is why a strong affiliation with school can be so valuable. The situation is far from hopeless; the future holds great promise for students who have strong connections to their school.

There is much reason to hope for the future. Two-thirds of students across the country already feel connected to their schools. Since 1994, the number of students engaging in unhealthy behaviors has been declining. In a 2004 press release, the Centers for Disease Control noted much less sexual activity, tobacco and alcohol use, and violence among high school students.

According to statistics from the 2003 Youth Risk Behavior Surveillance System, the number of students in physical fights dropped from 43 percent in 1991 to 33 percent in 2003. The number of high school students having sexual intercourse decreased from 54 percent in 1991 to 47 percent in 2003. In 2003, fewer students reported smoking cigarettes, from 36 percent in 1997 to 22 percent, and drinking alcohol, from 82 percent in 1991 to 75 percent (Centers for Disease Control, 2004).

Despite the declines, the dismal odds against young people persist. Even apparently well-connected students can be enticed to participate in dangerous behaviors. The task facing educators and parents can be daunting, but not impossible.

Although risky behaviors among adolescents are still too high, American schools are recommitting themselves to building relationships, raising achievement scores, and reducing violence. National, state, and local educational agencies are citing research into school connectedness and noting its implications for school policies. Additional, the good news is that school connectedness can be addressed without requiring a new or costly prevention program. In fact, many schools have already written school connectedness into their mission statements, safety plans, and system goals. While the term "school connectedness" may not be a household word yet, strong school connections are being fostered throughout the country.

Because many adolescent health risks overlap, developing a universal or schoolwide program reduces the threat of multiple risk factors in a cost-effective manner (Greenberg et al., 1999). The whole school approach involves commitment from everyone on the campus and extends benefits throughout the community. These types of programs promote resilience and mental health. A universal program designed to reach every student, not just a target group, can be an inexpensive yet effective approach to addressing the multitude of problems that undermine child development.

Strengthening relationships with adolescents will safeguard youth from engaging in unsafe behaviors. Strong school connections will also weaken the appeal of dangerous behaviors (Greenberg et al., 1999). Researchers warn educators not to minimize the simple and cost-effective approaches to intervention (Stoolmiller et al., 2000). McDonald and Wright (2002) also encourage administrators to explore factors in the school setting that contribute to alienation and antisocial behavior rather than focus on deviant behaviors.

When dealing with issues involving school commitment, bullying prevention will also require a comprehensive plan of action. Low school connectedness is predictive of bullying and victimization (Young, 2004). Weak school ties are also evidenced by a greater number of visits to the school nurse, cigarette use, and a lack of involvement in extracurricular activities (Bonny et al., 2000). The expense of not undertaking a plan to increase school ties will result in long-term, poor health outcomes associated with bullying, alienation, and disconnectedness.

The World Health Organization's Health Behavior in School-Aged Children Survey of 15,686 sixth- through tenth-grade students research suggests that boys in higher grades are more likely to disengage from school because of ongoing victimization and bullying (Nansel et al., 2001). While girls do engage in bullying, the aggression is most often exhibited socially through gossip, social isolation, and exclusion (Bonny et al., 2000; Ellickson and McGuigan, 2000). Social exclusion, peer isolation, and other relational forms of aggression frequently define the bullying behaviors of girls, yet these actions are no less harmful to the victims (Nansel et al., 2001; Smith et al., 1999).

Girls are often victimized by disparaging words that take a social and emotional toll on them (Harris et al., 2002). The cruelty of girls against each other often goes unnoticed by teachers due to the subtle nature of the behaviors (Casey-Cannon, Hayward, and Gowen, 2001). The impact of the social aggression, though, can contribute to increased absenteeism and poor academic performance (Casey-Cannon et al., 2001). Social forms of bullying also contribute to adolescent depression in girls (Bond, Carlin, Thomas, Rubin, and Patton, 2001).

Students with no school attachments are at great risk for continued violence. Victimization is inversely related to school attachment. My research study indicated that school connectedness predicted the presence and the levels of victimization. Stronger school ties were associated with a lower level of victimization or fear of bullying. Tenuous links to school were related to higher levels of victimization and bullying.

In light of the substantial research on the popularity of boys who bully, I wondered if school connectedness would be positively associated with bullying. I was certain that I would find victims to be alienated from school, but was not sure how well connected the bullies would be. My research revealed that limited school ties and lower school connectedness scores correlated with a high tendency to bully.

According to the study, bullies did not see themselves as having close relationships with either students or teachers. Voors (2000) also noted that bullies were less likely to feel a sense of belonging to school than those who did not engage in bullying behaviors. Similarly, alienation from school has been found to be strongly related to bullying behaviors (Dake et al., 2003). As a whole, perceptions of bullying and victimization were inversely correlated with school connectedness.

School connectedness is predictive of the levels of victimization and bullying. Students who had strong ties to school were the least likely to report high levels of victimization or to engage in bullying behaviors. Victims and bullies had the weakest affiliations to school, with victim aggressors experiencing the least amount of school connectedness. Previous findings also revealed that one of the top predictors of bullying is the tendency to be withdrawn or isolated (Viadero, 2003).

School connectedness is the strongest barrier to numerous at-risk behaviors for adolescents (Bonny et al., 2000). The strength of school connectedness reduces health risks from early sexual activity, sexual promiscuity, cigarette smoking, alcohol and drug use, violence, and other antisocial behaviors. These at-risk behaviors also have long-term mental and physical health consequences. By exploring school connectedness, researchers will continue to design additional measures that will deter bullying and other dangerous activities.

When schools explore the levels of connectedness on their campuses, scores from the School Connectedness Scale will expose the level of school connectedness, as well as the level of potential victimization and bullying. The students with lower scores will have a weak commitment to school and will more than likely be experiencing some level of bullying involvement. Khosropour and Walsh (2001) warn that asking students general questions might lead to under-reporting of bullying.

My study revealed a direct inverse relationship between perceptions of school connectedness and bullying. Mulvey and Cauffman (2001) noted that school commitment was an accurate predictor of violent behaviors in the school setting. Specific measures on bullying, like the Revised Olweus Bully/Victim Questionnaire, though, will help educators to ascertain specific details about the bullying problem, including where and how often it occurs. Generally, the alienation of bullies and victims is evident in their limited investment in school.

In the Alabama study, sixth grade students perceived the highest level of bullying, yet perceptions of school connectedness were the strongest among grades five through eight (Young, 2004). This finding suggested that some degree of bullying might be acceptable and, therefore, it did not interfere with the development of close relationships in school. Educators must continue to reject aggression as normative behavior. Further research should examine if, indeed, a threshold of bullying does exist and once that threshold is reached, if students begin to disengage.

Prevention should focus on reducing adult and peer acceptance of bullying behaviors. Pelligrini (2002) notes that adolescents hold more positive views of aggression than other age groups do. Aggression and the devastating consequences of bullying are too great to dismiss as a part of normal childhood development. Unfortunately, playground fights can no longer be seen as harmless scuffles. Now those incidents have the potential to erupt into deadly violence (Lamberg, 1998).

As adolescents make the transition to adulthood, their connections will provide stability or entice the young people to engage in risky behaviors. School connectedness will help adolescents build a sturdy bridge to adulthood; bullying makes those bridges fragile. Chandras (1999) describes the isolated adolescent's view of the world as more negative than that of other groups. Connecting with alienated adolescents will reduce their propensity for violence and other risky behaviors.

Researchers warn that the focus of prevention should not be too simplistic or narrow, by addressing victims and bullies as separate groups (Viadero, 2003). The lines between victimization and bullying sometimes blur, as when victims resort to violence. Although aggressive behaviors have actually been found to increase the popularity of middle school boys, bullies, in general, do not maintain close relationships in school (Espelage, Holt and Henkel, 2003). Bullying, however, is often witnessed by other students. In order for students to feel safe enough to condemn bullying, schools must foster a positive affiliation with students (Mulvey and Cauffman, 2001).

With strong school connections, adolescents become less vulnerable to violence, smoking, early sexual activity, alcohol, drugs, truancy, and delinquency. The Centers for Disease Control and Prevention (2001) notes that, regardless of ethnic, socioeconomic, religious, or sexual orientation, students who feel connected to school are more likely to do well, and less likely to engage in delinquent behaviors. Delinquent and risk-taking behaviors increase the risk for injury, which is the leading cause of death for youth (Pickett et al., 2002).

Bonny et al. (2000) suggest that researchers investigate the individual characteristics of students who have the highest levels of school connectedness. Identifying these characteristics will help educators develop individualized programs that instill these characteristics in all students. Students with high levels of school connectedness are less prone to academic problems, as well as mental and physical health problems. Other worthwhile research may include studies involving the ages at which intervention and building school connectedness are most effective.

Schools have the tools to discourage bullying through intervention and prevention efforts that also build school connectedness. Forging strong bonds with students will greatly reduce the consequences of victimization and bullying behaviors. Educators and parents should strengthen ties to students by reaching out to all young people. School connectedness provides long-term health benefits for students and should be a part of every bullying prevention program.

Collaboration among schools, families, and communities offers the best chance of building connections with children and preventing school violence (Evans and Rey, 2001). As Mulvey and Cauffman

(2001) point out, school violence does not occur within a vacuum. Educators must recognize that communities and schools have a mutual interest in preventing aggressive behavior. Addressing bullying will reduce school violence; however, prevention requires a strong commitment among educators, parents, community members, and students (Spivak and Prothrow-Stith, 2001).

Many school systems have developed plans that incorporate school connectedness as a part of their safety plans. Teachers must devise strategies to implement these plans. It is important to remember that simple strategies, such as making direct eye contact with students, offering more opportunities for students to be involved in school, having clear expectations, and listening to students make all the difference in the world in connecting with adolescents. We know that teachers will continue to do these things, no matter how many demands are made on them. The hope for the future is that the focus will remain on connecting with students.

Although school connectedness is not a panacea, young people have a greater chance of success when they have strong ties to school. Increasingly, middle school educators can take advantage of training opportunities that will help them address the special needs of adolescents. In addition, more organizations and educational initiatives are offering supportive programs for those who work with this unique population. School connectedness is the best hope against multiple at-risk factors for adolescents (Bonny et al., 2000).

Building school connectedness will not eliminate violence from school campuses. It is no guarantee that alcohol and drug use will not occur, nor will it end delinquency and early sexual activity. The incidence of these anti-social behaviors, though, will diminish as school connectedness increases. Complex problems require comprehensive plans of action. Strengthening school connectedness is the foundation on which to act. Connecting with young people today builds hope for the future.

References

Alspaugh, J. W. (1998). The relationship of school-to-school transitions and school size to high school dropout rates. *High School Journal, 81*, 154.

American Federation of Teachers. (2000). *Building from the Best, Learning from What Works: Five Promising Discipline and Violence Prevention Programs.* Washington, D.C.: American Federation of Teachers.

Anderson, M., Kaufman, J., Simon, T. R., Barrios, L., Paulozi, L., Ryan, G., Hammond, R., Modzeleski, W., Feucht, T., Potter, L., and the School-Associated Violent Death Group. (2001). School-associated violent deaths in the United States, 1994–1999. *Journal of the American Medical Association, 286*, 2695–2702.

Aronson, E. (2000). *Nobody Left to Hate: Teaching Compassion after Columbine.* New York: Worth Publishers.

Baer, J. (1999). Adolescent development and the junior high school environment. *Social Work in Education, 21*, 238.

Barnes, G. M., Welte, J. W., and Hoffman, J. H. (2002). Relationship of alcohol use to delinquency and illicit drug use in adolescents: gender, age, and racial/ethnic differences. *Journal of Drug Issues, 32*, 153.

Bearman, P. S., Jones, J., and Udry, J. R. (1997). The National Longitudinal Study of Adolescent Health: Research Design. Retrieved on June 26, 2001, from www.cpc.unc.edu/addhealth

Beier, S. R., Rosenfeld, W. D., Spitalny, K. C., Zansky, S. M., and Bontempo, A. N. (2000). The potential role of an adult mentor in influencing high-risk behaviors in adolescents. *Archives of Pediatrics & Adolescent Medicine, 154*, 327–331.

Blum, R. W., McNeely, C. A., and Rinehart, P. M. (2002). *Improving the odds: The untapped power of schools to improve the health of teens.*

Center for Adolescent Health and Development, University of Minnesota, Minneapolis, MN.

Bond, L., Carlin, J. B., Thomas, L., Rubin, K., and Patton, G. (2001). Does bullying cause emotional problems? A prospective study of young teenagers. *BMJ: British Medical Journal, 323.*

Bonny, A. E., Britto, M. T., Klostermann, B. K., Hornung, R. W., and Slap, G. B. (2000). School disconnectedness: Identifying adolescents at risk. *Pediatrics, 106,* 1017.

Borowsky, I. W. and Ireland, M. (2004). Predictors of future fight-related injury among adolescents. *Pediatrics, 113,* 530–536.

Borowsky, I. W., Ireland, M., and Resnick, M. D. (2001). Adolescent suicide attempts: Risks and protectors. *Predictors, 107,* 485.

Bowen, G. L., and Van Dorn, R. A. (2002). Community violent crime rates and school danger. *Children & Schools, 24.*

Bowman, D. H. (2002). Experts ponder Sept. 11 effect on school violence. *Education Week, 21,* 1.

Bracher, M. (2000). Adolescent violence and identity vulnerability. *Journal for the Psychoanalysis of Culture & Society, 5,* 189.

Brook, J., and Balka, E. B. (1999). The risks for late adolescence of early adolescent marijuana use. *American Journal of Public Health, 89,* 1549.

Burns, J. M., Andrews, G., and Szabo, M. (2002). Depression in young people: What causes it and can we prevent it? *Medical Journal of Australia, 177,* S93–S96. Retrieved on December 30, 2002, from www.mja.com.au/public/issues/177_07_071002/bur10371_fm.html

Casey-Cannon, S., Hayward, C., and Gowen, K. (2001). Middle-school girls' reports of peer victimization: Concerns, consequences, and implications. *Professional School Counseling, 5,* 138.

Centers for Disease Control and Prevention. (2001). School health guidelines to prevent unintentional injuries and violence. *Morbidity and Mortality Weekly Report, 50* (RR-22).

Centers for Disease Control and Prevention. (2002). *CDC Research Agenda—Preventing Youth Violence.* National Center for Injury Prevention and Control.

Centers for Disease Control and Prevention. (2004). Despite improvements, many high school students still engaging in risky health behaviors. *Press Release.* National Center for Chronic Disease Prevention and Health Promotion.

Center for the Study and Prevention of Violence. (1999). *Social Contexts and Adolescent Violence, Fact Sheet No. 8.* Retrieved on June 4, 2001, from www.colorado.edu/cspv/factsheets/factsheet8.html

Center for the Study and Prevention of Violence. (2001). *Youth Crime Prevention and Intervention: Comprehensive Evaluation Plan*. Retrieved on June 4, 2001, from www.colorado.edu/cspv/ycpi/CEP/navigate.htm

Center for the Study and Prevention of Violence. (2001). *Youth Crime Prevention and Intervention: Health and Asset Models*. Retrieved on June 4, 2001, from www.colorado.edu/cspv/ycpi/CEP/navigate.htm

Chandras, K. V. (1999). Coping with adolescent school violence: Implications for counseling. *College Student Journal, 33,* 302.

Ciampi, D. (2001). Perpetrators of violence: Adolescents in America. *The Forensic Examiner, 9,* 31.

Colangelo, N., Assouline, S. G., and Gross, M. U. M. (Eds.). (2004). *A Nation Deceived: How Schools Hold Back America's Brightest Students, Volume I.* Iowa City, Iowa: The Connie Belin and Jacqueline N. Blank International Center for Gifted Education and Talent Development.

Colangelo, N., Assouline, S. G., and Gross, M. U. M. (Ed.). (2004). *A Nation Deceived: How Schools Hold Back America's Brightest Students, Volume II.* Iowa City, Iowa: The Connie Belin and Jacqueline N. Blank International Center for Gifted Education and Talent Development.

Colvin, G., Tobin, T., Beard, K., Hagan, S., and Sprague, J. (1998). The school bully: Assessing the problem, developing interventions, and future research directions. *Journal of Behavioral Education, 8* (3), 293–319.

Cooke, B. (n.d.). Your teen's brain: It really is different! *Family Education.* Retrieved on August 21, 2004, from www.familyeducation.com/article/0,1120,21-18205,00.html

Cooper, W. O., Lutenbacher, M., and Faccia, K. (2000). Components of effective youth violence prevention programs for 7- to 14-year olds. *Archives of Pediatrics & Adolescent Medicine, 154,* 1134.

Dake, J. A., Price, J. H., and Telljohann, S. K. (2003). The nature and extent of bullying at school. *Journal of School Health, 73,* 173.

Desimone, L. (1999). Linking parent involvement with student achievement. *The Journal of Educational Research, 93,* 11.

DuRant, R. H., Kahn, J., Beckford, P. H., Woods, E. R. (1997). The association of weapon carrying and fighting on school property and other health risk and problem behaviors among high school students. *Archives of Pediatrics & Adolescent Medicine, 151,* 360.

DuRant, R. H., Krowchuk, D. P., Kreiter, S., Sinal, S. H., and Woods, C. R. (1999). Weapon carrying on school property among middle school students. *Archives of Pediatrics & Adolescent Medicine, 153,* 21.

Dwyer, K. P. (1999). Children killing children: Strategies to prevent youth violence. *Communique, Spring, Special Edition,* 1.

Dwyer, K., Osher, D., and Warger, C. (1998). *Early Warning, Timely Response: A Guide to Safe Schools*. Washington, D.C.: U.S. Department of Education.

Eaton, D. K., Forthofer, M. S., Zapata, L. B., Brown, K. R., Bryant, C. A., Reynolds S. T., and McDermott, R. J. (2004). Factors related to alcohol use among 6th through 10th graders: The Sarasota County demonstration project. *Journal of School Health, 74,* 95–104.

Eckman, A. (2001). Beyond bullying: Knowing when to step in and when not to. *Education Update, 43,* 1.

Eisenberg, M. E., Neumark-Sztainer, D., and Perry, C. L. (2003). Peer harassment, school connectedness, and academic achievement. *Journal of School Health, 73,* 311–316.

Ellickson, P. L., and McGuigan, K. A. (2000). Early predictors of adolescent violence. *The American Journal of Public Health, 90,* 566.

Espelage, D. L., Bosworth, K., Simon, T. R. (2000). Examining the social context of bullying behaviors in early adolescence. *Journal of Counseling & Development, 78,* 326.

Espelage, D. L., Holt, M. K., and Henkel, R. R. (2003). Examination of peer-group contextual effects on aggression during early adolescence. *Child Development, 74,* 205–220.

Evans, G. D., and Rey, J. (2001). In the echoes of gunfire: Practicing psychologists' responses to school violence. *Professional Psychology: Research & Practice, 32.*

Flannery, D. J., and Singer, M. I. (1999). Exposure to violence and victimization at school. *Choices Briefs, 4.*

Garbarino, J., and de Lara, E. (2002). *And Words Can Hurt Forever.* New York: Simon & Schuster.

Grant, S. H., Van Acker, R., Guerra, N., Duplechain, R., and Coen, M. (1998). A school and classroom enhancement program to prevent the development of antisocial behavior in children from high-risk neighborhoods. *Preventing School Failure, 42,* 121.

Greenberg, M. T., Domitrovich, C., and Bumbarger, B. (1999). *Preventing Mental Disorders in School-Age Children: A Review of the Effectiveness of Prevention Programs.* University Park, PA: Prevention Research for the Promotion of Human Development.

Harris, S. L., and Lowery, S. (2002). A view from the classroom. *Educational Leadership, 59,* 64.

Harris, S., Petrie, G., and Willoughby, W. (2002). Bullying among 9th graders: An exploratory study, *National Association of Secondary School Principals Bulletin, 86.*

Harrison, P. A. and Narayan, G. (2003). Differences in behavior, psychological factors, and environmental factors associated with participation in school sports and other activities in adolescence. *Journal of School Health, 73,* 113–20.

Hawkins, J. D., Catalano, R. F., Kosterman, R., Abbott, R., and Hill, K. G. (1999). Preventing adolescent health-risk behaviors by strengthening protection during childhood. *Archives of Pediatrics & Adolescent Medicine, 153,* 226.

Hazler, R. J. (2000). When victims turn aggressors: Factors in the development of deadly school violence. *Professional School Counseling, 4.*

Henry, D., Guerra, N., Huesmann, R., Tolan, P., VanAcker, P., and Eron, P. (2000). Normative influences on aggression in urban classrooms. *American Journal of Community Psychology, 28,* 59.

Henze, R. C. (2001). Segregated classrooms, integrated intent: How one school responded to the challenge of developing positive interethnic relations. *Journal of Education for Students Placed At-Risk, 6,* 133–155.

Hill, S. C., and Drolet, J. C. (1999). School-related violence among high school students in the United States, 1993–1995. *Journal of School Health, 69,* 264.

Holtappels, H. G., and Meier, U. (2000). Violence in schools. *European Education, 32,* 66.

Hoang, F. Q. (2001). Addressing school violence. *FBI Law Enforcement Bulletin, 70,* 18.

Jaffe, M. L. (1998). *Adolescence.* New Jersey: John Wiley & Sons.

Junge, S. K., Manglallan, S., and Raskauskas, J. (2003). Building life skills through after-school participation in experiential and cooperative learning. *Child Study Journal, 33,* 165–174.

Kallestad, J. H., Olweus, D., and Alsaker, F. (1998). School climate reports from Norwegian teachers: A methodological and substantive study. *School Effectiveness and School Improvement, 9,* 70–94.

Kaltiala-Heino, R., Rimpela, M., Rantanen, P., and Rimpela, A. (2000). Bullying at school—an indicator of adolescents at risk for mental disorders. *Journal of Adolescence, 23,* 661–674.

Karcher, M. J. and Lee, Y. (2002). Connectedness among Taiwanese middle school students: A validation study of the Hemingway measure of adolescent connectedness. *Asian Pacific Education Review, 3,* 92–114.

Kellam, S. G. (2002). Why the prevention of aggressive disruptive behaviors in middle school must begin in elementary schools. *The Clearing House, 72,* 242–245.

Khosropour, S. C., and Walsh, J. (2001). *That's Not Teasing—That's Bullying: A Study of Fifth Graders' Conceptualization of Bullying and Teasing. Bullying in Schools.* Paper presented at the Annual Conference of the American Educational Research Association. Retrieved October 12, 2001, from ERIC/ CASS Virtual Library. http://ericcass.uncg.edu/virtuallib/bullying/1065.html

Kimmel, M. S., and Mahler, M. (2003). Adolescent masculinity, homophobia, and violence. *American Behavioral Scientist, 46,* 1439–1458.

King, A., Vidourek, R. A., Davis, B., and McClellan, W. (2002). Increasing self-esteem and school connectedness through a multidimensional mentoring program. *Journal of School Health, 72.*

Kodjo, C. M., Auinger, P., and Ryan, S. A. (2003). Demographic, intrinsic, and extrinsic factors associated with weapon carrying at school. *Archives of Pediatrics & Adolescent Medicine, 157,* 96–103.

Kumpulainen, K., Rasanen, E., and Puura, K. (2001). Psychiatric disorders and the use of mental health services among children involved in bullying. *Aggressive Behavior, 27,* 102–110.

Lamberg, L. (1998). Preventing school violence: No easy answers. *Journal of the American Medical Association, 280,* 5.

Landau, M. (2001). Deciphering the adolescent brain. *The Harvard University Gazette, 4/21.*

Lane-Garon, P. S. (2000). Practicing peace: The impact of a school-based conflict resolution program on elementary students. *Peace & Change, 25,* 467.

Lepore, C. and Bobinchock, A. (2003). Adolescent stress can change brain during development. *McLean Hospital, 1108.* Retrieved on September 4, 2004, from www.mclean.harvard.edu/PublicAffairs/adolstress20031108 .html

Lerner, R. M. and Galambos, N. L. (1998). Adolescent development: Challenges and opportunities for research, programs, and policies. *Annual Review of Psychology, 49,* 413–446.

Lerner, R. M., Lerner, J. V., DeStefanis, I., and Apfel, A. (2001). Understanding developmental systems in adolescence: Implications for methodological strategies, data analytic approaches, and training. *Journal of Adolescent Research, 16,* 9.

Levin-Epstein, M. (Ed.) (2003) Bullying: A comprehensive approach to prevention. *Inside School Safety.*

Li, X., Howard, D., Stanton, B., Rachuba, L., and Cross, S. (1998). Distress symptoms among urban African American children and adolescents. *Archives of Pediatrics & Adolescent Medicine, 152,* 569–577.

MacDonald, M., and Wright, N. E. (2002). Cigarette smoking and the disenfranchisement of adolescent girls: A discourse of resistance. *Health Care for Women International, 23,* 281–305.

Marshall, M. C. (2000). From the inside looking out: Violence in schools. *Journal of Child & Adolescent Psychiatric Nursing, 13,* 133.

Mather, V. (2001). Building a nonviolent culture for learning. *Reclaiming Children and Youth, 9,* 202.

McEvoy, A., and Welker, R. (2000). Antisocial behavior, academic failure, and school climate: A critical review. *Journal of Emotional & Behavioral Disorders, 8,* 130.

McNeal, Jr., R. B. (2001). Differential effects of parental involvement on cognitive and behavioral outcomes by socioeconomic status. *Journal of Socio-Economics, 30,* 171.

McNeely, C. *Connection to school as an indicator of positive development.* Paper presented for the Indicators of Positive Development Conference, March 12–13, 2003, Washington, D.C.

McNeely, C. A., Nonnemaker, J. M., and Blum, R. W. (2002). Promoting school connectedness: Evidence from the National Longitudinal Study of Adolescent Health. *Journal of School Health, 72,* 138–146.

Morrison, K. (2001). Challenges and opportunities in education. *Adolescent & Family Health.* Retrieved on July 3, 2002, from www.afhjournal.org/features/010205.htm

Mulvey, E. P., and Cauffman, E. (2001). The inherent limits of predicting school violence. *American Psychologist, 56,* 10.

Mytton, J. A., DiGuiseppi, C., Gough, D. A., Taylor, R. S., and Logan, S. (2002). School-based violence prevention programs. *Archives of Pediatrics & Adolescent Medicine, 156,* 752–762.

Nansel, T. R., Overpeck, M. D., Haynie, D. L., Ruan, W. J., and Scheidt, P. C. (2003). Relationships between bullying and violence among U.S. youth. *Archives of Pediatrics & Adolescent Medicine, 157,* 348–353.

Nansel, T. R., Overpeck, M., Pilla, R. S., Ruan, W. J., Simons-Morton, B., and Scheidt, P. (2001). Bullying behaviors among U.S. youth: Prevalence and association with psychosocial adjustment. *JAMA, Journal of the American Medical Association, 285.* 2094.

National Institute of Mental Health (NIMH). (2000). *Child and Adolescent Violence Research, Publication No. 00-4706.* Bethesda, MD: Department of Health and Human Services.

National Institute of Mental Health (NIMH). (2000). *Helping Children and Adolescents Cope with Violence and Disasters.* Bethesda, MD: Department of Health and Human Services

National School Safety Center. (1998). *Checklist of Characteristics of Youth Who Have Caused School-Associated Deaths.* Retrieved on July 22, 2004, from www.nssc1.org/reporter/checklist.htm

National Strategy for Suicide Prevention. (2002). Retrieved on July 3, 2002, from www.mentalhealth.org/suicideprevention/young.asp

Natvig, G. K., Albrektsen, G., and Qvarnstrom, U. (2001). School-related stress experience as risk factor for bullying behavior. *Journal of Youth and Adolescence, 30,* 561.

Novotney, L. C., Mertinko, E., Lange, J., Falb, T., and Kirk, H. (2002). Juvenile mentoring program: Early evaluation results suggest promise of benefits for youth. *Information Technology International Bulletin.*

Olsen, L. (2002). Detachment starts in middle school. *Education Week,* May 29.

Olweus, D. (1993). *Bullying at School.* Oxford, UK: Blackwell Publishers Ltd.

Olweus, D. (2003). A profile of bullying. *Educational Leadership,* March 12–17.

Olweus, D., Limber, S., and Mihalic, S. F. (1999). *Blueprints for Violence Prevention, Book Nine: Bullying Prevention Program.* Boulder, CO: Center for the Study and Prevention of Violence.

Otten, E. H. (2000). Character education. *ERIC Digest. ED No. ED444932.* Bloomington, IN: ERIC Clearinghouse for Social Studies/Social Science Education.

Pelligrini, A. D. (2002). Bullying, victimization, and sexual harassment during the transition to middle school. *Educational Psychologist, 37,* 151–163.

Peterson, R. L., and Skiba, R. (2001). Creating school climates that prevent school violence. *Social Studies, 92,* 167.

Pickett, W., Schmidt, H., Boyce, W. F., Simpson, K., Scheidt, P. C., Mazur, J., Molcho, M., King, M. A., Godeau, E., Overpeck, Aszmann, A., Szabo, M., Harel, Y. (2002). Multiple risk behavior and injury. *Archives of Pediatrics & Adolescent Medicine,* 156.

Price, J. H., Telljohann, S. K., Dake, J. A., Marsico, L., and Zyla, C. (2002). Urban elementary school students' perceptions of fighting behavior and concerns for personal safety. *Journal of School Psychology, 72,* 184.

Renzulli, J. and Park, S. (2002). *Giftedness and High School Dropouts: Personal, Family, and School-related Factors* (RM02168). Storrs, Connecticut: The National Research Center on the Gifted and Talented, University of Connecticut.

Scales, P. C. (2000). Building student's developmental assets to promote health and school success. *Clearing House, 74,* 84.

Shidler, L. (2001). Teacher-sanctioned violence. *Childhood Education, 77,* 167.

Smith, P. K., Morita, Y., Junger-Tas, J., Olweus, D., Catalano, R., and Slee, P. (Eds.). (1999). *The Nature of School Bullying: A Cross-National Perspective.* NY: Routledge.

Spinks, S. (2002). Adolescent brains are works in progress: Here's why. *Frontline*. Retrieved on August 21, 2004, from www.pbs.org/wgbh/pages/frontline/shows/teenbrain/work/adolescent.html

Spivak, H., and Prothrow-Stith, D. (2001). The need to address bullying—an important component of violence prevention. (Editorial). *JAMA, The Journal of the American Medical Association, 285*, 2131.

Stephens, R. D. (1999). Director's update: Top 10 strategies for schools to consider in the wake of the Colorado shootings. *School Safety Update, 5*, 1.

Stoolmiller, M., Eddy, J. M., and Reid, J. B. (2000). Detecting and describing preventive intervention effects in a universal school-based randomized trial targeting delinquent and violent behavior. *Journal of Consulting and Clinical Psychology, 68*, 296–306.

Substance Abuse. (2002). *National Youth Violence Prevention Resource Center*. Retrieved on July 3, 2002, from www.safeyouth.org

Tani, F., Greenman, P. S., Schneider, B. H., and Fregoso, M. (2003). Bullying and the big five. *School Psychology International, 24*, 131–146.

Taylor, H. E. and Larson, S. (1999). Social and emotional learning in middle school. *The Clearing House, 72*, 331.

Thomas, H. (1997). *The Shame Response to Rejection*. Sewickley, PA: Albanel Publishers.

United States Department of Health and Human Services. (2000). *Youth Violence: A Report of the Surgeon General*. Atlanta, GA: Centers for Disease Control and Prevention.

Unnever, J. D., and Cornell, D. G. (2003). Bullying, self-control, and ADHD. *Journal of Interpersonal Violence, 18*, 129–147.

Van der Wal, M. F., de Wit, C. A. M., and Hirasing, R. A. (2003). Psychosocial health among young victims and offenders of direct and indirect bullying. *Pediatrics, 111*, 1312–1317.

Vander Zanden, J. W. (2000). *Human Development, 7th Edition*. Boston, MA: McGraw-Hill Higher Education.

Viadero, D. (2003). Research: Tormentors. *Education Week, 22*, 24.

Voors, W. (2000). *The Parent's Book About Bullying: Changing the Course of Your Child's Life*. Center City, MN: Hazelden.

Weinstein, C., Curran, M., and Tomlinson-Clarke, S. (2003). Culturally responsive classroom management: Awareness into action. *Theory into Practice, 42*, 269–276.

Weir, E. (2001). The health impact of bullying. *CMAJ: Canadian Medical Association Journal, 165*.

Why do some people drink too much? (2000). *Alcohol Research & Health, 24*, 17–26.

Willert, H. J. (2002). Do sweat the small stuff: Stemming school violence. *American Secondary Education, 30,* 2–13.

Winter, M. (2001). Safe Schools. *Human Ecology,* 29, *1,* 21.

Young, D. H. (2004). School connectedness predicts bullying: An analysis of perceptions among middle school students. *Journal of At-Risk Issues, 10,* 29–40.

Zeedyk, H. S., Gallacher, J., Henderson, M., Hope, G., Husband, B., and Lindsay, K. (2003). Negotiating the transition from primary to secondary school. *School Psychology International, 24,* 67–79.

Index

About the Author

Dr. Deana H. Young has an extensive background working with adolescents. At the age of twenty, she began working with troubled teens as a volunteer. Following graduation from college, Dr. Young continued her work with children and their families in the social services and mental health fields. From directing a shelter for homeless women and children to her current work as a public school counselor, the author draws from her own experiences as a parent and educator to advocate for children of all ages.

Her research on school connectedness and bullying was published in the *Journal of At-Risk Issues, 10,* 2. Connecting with adolescents in school has been her passion on which she presented at the 16th Annual National Dropout Prevention Conference in Orlando, Florida. Other research areas of interest for the author include foster care and violence prevention.

www.ingramcontent.com/pod-product-compliance
Lightning Source LLC
Chambersburg PA
CBHW030656270326
41929CB00007B/394